What others are saying about this book:

 "BEST COOKBOOK OF THE YEAR" - N.A.B.E. Award

....*a feast, an opportunity to indulge in wonderful-tasting food without pangs of guilt.* - Barbara Hansen, LOS ANGELES TIMES.

...*a treasure trove...* - Sally Estes, BOOKLIST

Those who think heart-healthy diets must be bland, meager, and dull should make their way to this book post-haste....Only the French can compete when it comes to making vegetables delicious, only here India has the health advantage. - Susan Waggoner, SMALL PRESS MAGAZINE

The book is a masterpiece... - L.A. INDIA

INDIAN FOOD - an ancient system of cooking that is absolutely PERFECT - beautiful, fragrant spices enhancing wonderful vegetables, legumes, fruit, yoghurt - etc. etc. Suddenly, figuring out how to make nutritious meals is not perplexing anymore....Congratulations on your wonderful accomplishments. I hope you'll write even more books! I'll be the first in line to buy them. - A non-Indian reader

Spice up your menu....Indian cuisine is based on the ancient medical science, Ayurveda, which teaches that a healthy diet is essential for disease prevention. Lakhani takes the best of healthful Indian cuisine and makes it even better... - DELICIOUS! Magazine

What makes this book so unique and practical is that each recipe is followed by a nutrient analysis table....Such information is practically nonexistent for Indian recipes. - Francis Assisi, INDIA WEST

"Indian Cookbook Shows Ways To Add Years, Spice To Your Life." - Headline, LAS CRUCES BULLETIN

.......*continued overleaf*

Food Exchange Information for Diabetics
Many readers of earlier printings of this book have requested Food Exchange information for recipes in the book.
We are pleased to inform readers .... is now available. Please see page 287 for this inform

D1173118

Indian Recipes for a Healthy Heart

LOW-FAT

LOW-CHOLESTEROL

LOW-SODIUM GOURMET DISHES

from the Kitchen of

Mrs. Lakhani

FAHIL PUBLISHING COMPANY
LOS ANGELES

Indian Recipes for a Healthy Heart

In writing this book, the author has used reliable current information from sources quoted in the book. However, there may be some inconsistencies because of the nutrient variations in foods. Nothing contained in this book should be construed as a diet recommended by the author. Readers should not attempt to gain or lose weight or treat health conditions through diet or otherwise without consulting a physician.

To order copies of this book, please use the order form on page 287 or write to:
Fahil Publishing Company, Suite 310, P.O.Box 7000
Palos Verdes Peninsula, CA 90274 U.S.A.

Library of Congress Catalog Card Number: 91-092185
International Standard Book Number 0-9630235-0-0

Printed in the United States of America
First Printing 1991
Second Printing 1995, revised
Third Printing 1998

Contents

Recipes

For Your Information

Acknowledgements

Writing a cookery book is an arduous process at any time. Writing a cookery book which requires recipes to be modified, analyzed, tested and tasted repeatedly until an acceptable result is produced is a mammoth task which, at times, seemed as if it would never end. Such a task needed both a great deal of help and patience from everybody around me. My sincere gratitude is due:

To my husband, who throughout this project has been a dear friend and guide, a source of courage and support, and a helper in more ways than I can possibly write here. He has spent many hours helping with the editing and production of this book, and without his quiet but continuous encouragement this book may never have come to pass.

To my son and daughter, who have suffered the role of being 'guinea-pigs' while I have been developing these recipes. I reasoned that if my recipes passed muster of these two adolescents, who had been weaned on traditional Indian and European cuisine, and who tend to be very particular about their food, then the recipes were fit for publication.

To my father and mother, who inculcated in me the virtues of home cooking, and who had insisted when I was young, and probably not terribly keen, that I should learn the art of Indian cooking. I am particularly indebted to my mother who taught me most of what I know about cooking and providing nourishment for my family.

And finally to Dr. Kaushik, Dr. Platt and Dr. Rahimtoola -- three very eminent cardiologists who gave their very valuable time to read the manuscript and write forewords for this book, giving three different perspectives, which, between them, truly reflect the essence of the intent behind this book. My special gratitude is due to Dr. Kaushik who not only read the manuscript, but also checked all the facts and figures therein, and provided many helpful suggestions. My acknowledgements would not be complete without expressing thanks to Marlys Kinnel for her kind words and many helpful suggestions.

Foreword

Of all the ailments which may blow out life's little candle,
heart disease is the chief.

William Boyd

Diseases of the heart and blood vessels account for more than 45 percent of all deaths in the United States — many of them prematurely. One in every three men is likely to develop heart disease before the age of 60 years. Atherosclerosis (hardening of the arteries) and hypertension (high blood pressure) account for a large majority of these patients. There is an extensive body of scientific data linking cholesterol to atherosclerosis. Not only is high cholesterol associated with heart disease, but lowering of cholesterol reduces the risk of atherosclerosis as well. In fact, there is convincing evidence coming out that major reduction of blood cholesterol can result in regression of the hardening of arteries. Physicians have been recommending diets low in fat content for a few decades but it is a recent phenomena that the average American has become conscious of various fats in his/her diet. This changing trend in our culture needs to dissipate more widely and the efforts of American Heart Association, National Cholesterol Education Program, American Medical Association and others like the author of this book should be applauded.

Migration studies have shown that Japanese living in Japan have lower levels of cholesterol than Japanese living in the United States. There is a corresponding increase in atherosclerosis heart disease among these migrants. It appears that the same is true for migrants from the Indian Subcontinent. In my practice of cardiology I encounter a significant number of these migrants who could benefit from better control of their lipids and hypertension. Standard recipes available in most physician and dietitian offices do not appeal to their taste. That makes compliance very difficult, especially among the group that has not yet manifested the consequences of atherosclerosis or hypertension. Some of my patients have practically given up red meat and are constantly looking for vegetarian alternatives to continue enjoying the pleasure of healthy meals. This book, *Indian Recipes for a Healthy Heart*, is a God sent gift to many physicians like me and a multitude of patients. It is an extensively researched cook book. Mrs. Lakhani's recipes provide detailed information on calories, fats, types of fat and sodium content. Such information is rare to find in routine recipes and practically non-existent for these exotic dishes. I have personally tasted many of the dishes and find them very appealing to my amateurish gourmet taste. Now we can truly savor the Step 1/Step 2 American Heart Association diets.

William Shakespeare's dictum that "They are as sick that surfeit with too much, as they that starve with nothing" is as valid today as it was when he wrote *The Merchant of Venice*. To our patients, potential victims and healers of cardiac ailments Mrs. Lakhani's book which emphasizes moderation at all levels is a wish come true. I am so proud that a dear friend has, with her hard work and commitment to help her fellow beings, come forward to fill this significant void in our therapeutic armamentarium. Enjoy the delectable dishes in this book and beat the odds of being another statistical blip on the cardiac epidemiologist's graph.

Vidya S. Kaushik, M.D., D.M., (Card), F.A.C.C.

Interim Chairman
Department of Medicine and Cardiology
Charles R. Drew University of Medicine and Sciences
Los Angeles, California

Past President
American Heart Association, Greater Los Angeles Affiliate

Foreword

As a practicing cardiologist I first met Mrs. Lakhani when her husband was diagnosed with severe coronary artery disease. At that time it seemed obvious to me that as with a multitude of previous patients, this family would at first struggle with the reality of progressive heart disease and then succumb to the perceived inevitability of their fate. In this respect, all the habits of indulgent lifestyles would be reclaimed and further reinforced as a just reward for suffering and anguish.

To be fair, it is understandable that my foreshortened dietary instruction and the monotonous diatribe of published dietary literature did little to convince this woman that her husband's disease could truly be reversed. In this respect, the appeal of instant gratification through surgery or coronary angioplasty seems far more attractive than the monotony of an ordered existence and a bland diet.

To my great surprise the book that Mrs. Lakhani has written is a glimpse into a gifted and loving mother teaching her very stubborn clan the wondrous excitement associated with the process of true healing. In order to accomplish this aim, she has created some harmony amid the multitudes of contradictory claims and assertions that have flooded our society. For example she exposes the absurdity of manufacturers claims of "low cholesterol" products by a diligent and academic understanding of nutritional science. Additionally, she gives equal importance to lifestyle changes which she correctly perceives as a major factor in the progressive nature of coronary disease in our society. In this respect, she leads those who read and understand her book into the notion that healing takes collective and comprehensive changes which comes from the family and the heart. Thus, her book offers a glimpse into nurturing and feeding of the spirit and body in order to reverse the threat to one's existence.

For me as an individual only knowledgeable about Indian cooking from brief encounters at local restaurants, the range of foods and exciting presentation offers an avenue for exciting spices and exotic adventures. The analysis of nutritional value and relative cost in cholesterol, calories, carbohydrate and fat is truly a novel and effective approach to healthy dietary practice. Personally, I know of no other book which so accurately and practically presents these highly complex concepts. If one takes the time to embrace and understand these recipes for living then just as the exotic spices excite the palate, the daily chores of cooking can become meaningful attempts at bettering ones chances for survival.

However, in the last analysis, I feel that if Mrs. Lakhani had not written such a scholarly work, she could not have achieved the legitimacy she deserves. This book truly approaches the reality of coronary artery disease and makes accurate and practical suggestions which can be trusted and utilized on a daily basis. As a reference for Indian cuisine I can only guess at it's quality; as a reference for accurate and measured intake of food and life, this book is a masterpiece by a very loving mother and nurturer of her family.

Marc L. Platt, M.D.

Staff Cardiologist
Torrance Memorial Medical Center

Foreword

Coronary artery disease and hypertension (high blood pressure) are two major cardiovascular disorders in the developed countries. Persons whose origin is from Bangladesh, India, Pakistan, and Sri Lanka and reside in the western world (for example, in the U.S.A.) are not only not immune from these two disorders but in fact appear to develop coronary heart disease at a young age. In order to prevent, or at least to delay, the occurrence of these disorders, it is extremely important to take appropriate preventive measures.

For those who have hypertension or have a family history of hypertension, it would be wise to reduce the intake of sodium. Preventive measures for coronary artery disease means reducing the intake of cholesterol and fat; fat converts in the body to cholesterol. This advice is easy to come by but it is very difficult to achieve, particularly for those who largely eat food prepared according to their country of origin.

Mrs. Lakhani's book *Indian Recipes for a Healthy Heart* fills this gap. It contains recipes, and also, important and easy to understand guides to food constituents and a wealth of additional useful advise. It is highly recommended.

Shahbudin H. Rahimtoola, M.B., F.R.C.P.

George C. Griffith Professor of Cardiology
Professor of Medicine
Chief, Division of Cardiology
University of Southern California

Wisdom through the Ages

"Not life, but good life, is to be chiefly valued."
        –Socrates (469? - 399 B.C.)

"Moderation in everything except virtue."
        –A Greek philosopher.

"In those days again, it was lack of food that drove fainting bodies to death, now contrariwise it is the abundance that overwhelms them."
        –Lucretius (55 B.C.)

"There are two benefits of which the generality of man are losers, and of which they do not know the value, health and leisure."
        –Anonymous (circa 700 A.D.)

"A good kitchen, is a good Apothecaries shop."
        –William Bullein (d. 1576)

"Doctors are always working to preserve our health and cooks to destroy it, but the latter are the more often successful."
        –Denis Dierot (1713 - 1784)

"The Chinese do not draw any distinction between food and medicine."
        –Lin Yutang (1895 - 1976)

"One swears by wholemeal bread, or by sour milk; vegetarianism is the only road to salvation of some, others insist not only on vegetables above, but on eating those raw. At one time the only thing that matters is calories; at another time they are crazy about vitamins or about roughage.

    "The scientific truth may be put quite briefly; eat moderately, having an ordinary mixed diet, and don't worry."
        –Sir Robert Hutchinson (1932)

Introduction

An episode of a heart attack, bypass surgery, or even just the discovery of heart disease is a terrifying and traumatic experience for any family. A few years after my marriage we found out that my husband had high blood cholesterol. Our doctor gave him a handful of low-cholesterol, low-fat English recipes and a list of foods and ingredients he should eliminate from his diet. That is when the trouble started; the doctor's instructions eliminated a large part of our usual diet, which was mainly based on Indian and European cuisines. The recipes provided by the doctor were bland and lacked variety. The patient and the rest of the family rebelled against this deprivation. Not knowing any better, we reverted to our usual diet, but eliminated dishes which were obviously 'bad' -- those containing eggs, butter, cream, whole milk and all red meats, and we substituted margarine and vegetable oils for butter in our cooking. Now we felt only partially deprived. Still, we were happy in the thought that we were more or less following our doctor's advice.

Despite doing all this, a few years later my husband had to undergo bypass surgery following a sudden chest pain, but fortunately no heart attack. Our doctor said that my husband had been lucky, but he warned that another surgery in the future could not be ruled out unless we could lower his cholesterol level even further. This time around, the terror was complete and we knew that the time had come to take our diet even more seriously; but we still didn't know what to do.

I realized that there was nothing I could do about the past. But what I *could* do was to look after my family in a way that would help safeguard my husband's, my children's and my own health for the rest of our days. But how?

This was the beginning of my quest. I looked for a source of heart-healthy Indian recipes but could find none. So I decided that to succeed in my quest I really needed to understand what constituted the basis of a healthy diet -- why our previous diet had failed, and what was it about certain foods that resulted in diet-linked diseases. I started talking to doctors, to dietitians, and to nutritionists. I read all I could find.

I began to realize that our doctor's advice had not been incorrect, just incomplete; it was a matter of half knowledge being dangerous. We had known nothing about label reading, or what it meant when an acceptable vegetable oil was hydrogenated. I began to discover, for example, that all margarines are not created equal - some are even more dangerous than butter; that "100% cholesterol free" and many such packaging slogans on a label were by themselves not only meaningless but downright misleading. I also discovered that the quantities of certain food ingredients in our diet were as important as their quality. In hindsight, our diet had not been good enough. Another vital fact I discovered is that a good diet, although a very important factor, is not sufficient for achievement of good health -- other lifestyle factors such as exercise and stress management are equally, if not more, important. Our lifestyle had not been too good either.

It took me a long time to put the pieces together. On the food front I began to understand the importance of a total approach to diet rather than to individual dishes. I also realized that we need not have given up eating most of our favorite dishes, if I had only known how to render them healthful. There is nothing sacrosanct about classical recipes. This realization started the long process of experimentation and modification of recipes -- a process that required many trials before acceptable results were achieved; it also resulted in many a frustrating failure.

During my research I found that there were scores of people of Indian origin who were in the same situation as we. Many had been trying to live with patchy advice and recipes that they neither liked nor understood. Some were miserable, living on bland unbalanced diets. Others had long since given up and gone back to their original ways. There are many people in the Indian, Pakistani, Bangladeshi and Sri Lankan communities who have only known one kind of cuisine -- and that is Indian; and they would rather starve than switch to some foreign fare. The only concession that some of them have made to 'Western' food is the adoption of so called junk food -- doughnuts, hamburgers, pizzas and the like; they have sort of jumped from the frying pan into the fire. For all of them, the type of dietary advice they were given was of no help. Telling them about percentages of fat calories and milligrams of cholesterol per day had no meaning; they had no way of working out those things for their diet. They were just confused. What everybody simply wanted to know was exactly how to prepare *Indian foods* which met the recommended dietary guidelines.

In 1986, I was writing an Indian cookery book which was to have been a compilation of my favorite classical recipes. The experiences that I have described made me scrap that book entirely and write this book instead. This book is the result of my work in which I took classical Indian recipes (and a few non-Indian recipes in deference to our newly acquired tastes) and modified them so that they meet the current dietary guidelines for maintaining good health, such as those published by the American Heart Association. I have tried to modify them in such a way that the original tastes and flavors are largely maintained.

Since a proper diet is only one of the components in a healthy lifestyle, I have included additional information on subjects I consider important for understanding and achievement of a good level of overall fitness. I have tried to state things simply, in a lay person's language, in a way I wish they had been explained to me. I hope that readers of this book will find such additional information useful.

This book is primarily a cookbook. My main purpose in writing it is to help my family and other people who enjoy Indian food, or who would like to add variety to their diet, to live a healthy and fulfilling life -- food, after all, is a significant part of life's fulfillment. This book offers a set of favorite Indian recipes which meet current dietary guidelines for inclusion in a balanced diet. These recipes are designed to help healthy people stay healthy. Those who have medical conditions should be primarily guided by their physicians. However, they will find many recipes (and other information) which will help them implement the medical advice they are given. If you are not sure, please show this book to your dietitian and ask him or her to construct a suitable dietary plan for you, incorporating recipes from this book.

In this book I have explained the methods I have used to modify my recipes. You may find these explanations and other information useful in modifying your own favorite recipes to render them more healthful.

I have deliberately used a detailed step-by-step method to describe the preparation of every dish in the book. The purpose of this is to make it easier for readers who are new to Indian cooking, or indeed new to cooking, to obtain successful results.

I wish the readers of this book enjoyable eating, and a long and healthy life devoid of traumas brought about by the plague of modern silent killer diseases.

Postscript:

Ever since we started incorporating the recipes from this book into our family diet, both my husband and I have witnessed a drop in our cholesterol levels, we have lost weight, we feel better, and we have not once gone hungry or felt deprived. And our children still love the food at our table. These achievements alone have made all the effort worthwhile.

A Recipe for Overall Fitness

The Three Pillars of Overall Fitness

This is primarily a cookbook, with its main focus on a heart-healthy diet. However, a good balanced diet by itself does not guarantee overall fitness. Overall fitness can only be achieved through a balanced lifestyle in which diet is only one component. Some of the factors that affect our health are obviously not within our control, but the medical community is in overwhelming agreement that of the things human beings can do for themselves, three can make the greatest contribution towards achievement of all-round fitness: diet, exercise and stress management through balance in life.

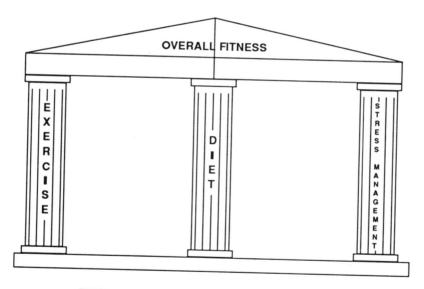

THREE PILLARS OF OVERALL FITNESS

This diagram illustrates the slab (Pediment) of 'Overall Fitness' resting on three pillars. The vertical line in the slab depicts a crack, signifying the fragility of fitness. Because of the crack, should any one of the pillars be removed, one or both the pieces of the slab will fall down and destroy the integrity of fitness.

The First Pillar - Balanced Diet

> *"In all, six of the ten leading causes of death in the United States have been linked to our diet."*
>
> Senator George McGovern, 1977

A balanced diet means eating a variety of foods so that the body receives the right amounts of the different nutrients that it needs. Unfortunately, this does not mean that we can eat equal amounts of all different types of foods. To make things easier, a number of simple guidelines are available.

The simplest way of explaining a balanced diet is through a simple graphical concept of a Healthy Diet Pyramid.

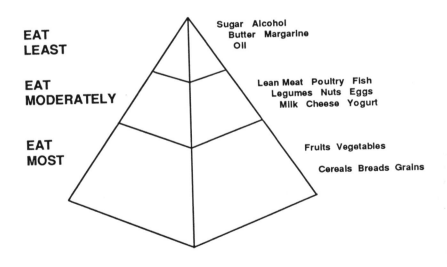

EAT LEAST — Sugar Alcohol Butter Margarine Oil

EAT MODERATELY — Lean Meat Poultry Fish Legumes Nuts Eggs Milk Cheese Yogurt

EAT MOST — Fruits Vegetables Cereals Breads Grains

HEALTHY DIET PYRAMID

The U.S. Department of Agriculture has divided food into five groups and has recommended the number of servings from each group to achieve a balanced diet. Please see explanation of servings on page 261.

Eat Most from:

Group 1.   Fruit and Vegetable Group
                4 or more servings per day
Group 2.   Grain Group: Breads, cereals and other grains
                4 or more servings per day

Eat Moderately from:

Group 3.   Milk Group: Milk and milk products
                Adults: 2 servings per day
                Children: 3 to 4 servings per day
                Pregnant and lactating women: 4 servings per day
Group 4.   Poultry, fish, meat, eggs, legumes, nuts and seeds
                2 servings per day

Eat least from:

Group 5.   Fats, Sugar, Sweets, and Alcohol
                No recommended number of servings

In addition, the American Heart Association has produced quantitative guidelines for food consumption based on nutritional values:

Nutrient	Recommended Consumption
Total Fat	Not more than 30% of total calories
Of which, Saturated Fat	Less than 10% of total calories*
Carbohydrates	50% to 60% of total calories
Protein	10% to 20% of total calories
Cholesterol	Less than 300 milligrams per day*
Calories	Enough to attain and maintain your ideal weight

*Please note: These recommendations are for healthy people. For persons who have elevated levels of blood cholesterol, it is recommended that less than 7% of total calories should be derived from saturated fat, and less than 200 milligrams of cholesterol be consumed daily. However, since each case is different, please be guided by your physician concerning your diet.

(Recipes in this book will allow you to construct dietary plans to meet the above guidelines. Please use the Nutrient Analysis given for each recipe and for some common foods on page 271 to assist you in diet planning. Please note that 1 gram fat equals 9 calories and 1 gram carbohydrates or protein equals 4 calories. Please also read "Analyzing Your Daily Diet" on page 263).

Cigarette Smoking

Cigarettes are never listed as being part of a diet. Yet for smokers they are as much a part of their diet as food is. I am therefore taking a writer's licence to include cigarettes in this category.

Amongst risk factors that people can do something about, smoking comes towards the top of the list. That smoking causes lung cancer and other disorders of the respiratory system is well known. What is perhaps not equally well known is that smoking is the prominent risk factor for heart attacks. Depending on how much you smoke your chances of suffering a heart attack may be doubled, tripled, or increased even more. On the other hand, if you quit smoking, the risk of heart attack returns to normal over a period of time.

The Second Pillar - Exercise

"Sedentary living, not cholesterol, is the nation's leading culprit in fatal heart attacks. Sedentary people are about twice as likely to die from coronary heart disease as people who are physically active"
Jane E. Brody New York Times, October 11, 1990

Recent research conducted in the United States and elsewhere has produced overwhelming evidence that regular exercise reduces both morbidity and incidence of premature death. One only has to consider some of the benefits of exercise to appreciate why this may be so:

Exercise
- strengthens the heart
- conditions lungs and the circulatory system
- reduces fat mass in the body
- reduces 'bad' (LDL) cholesterol
- increases 'good' (HDL) cholesterol
- lowers blood pressure
- reduces stress
- burns up calories and helps with weight control
- speeds up metabolism
- increases strength and stamina
- makes you feel better in body and mind
- helps in preventing and/or alleviating some diseases

To most people exercise conjures up visions of lengthy and tiring workouts in a gym or on a track, or playing some exhausting sport. It is good if you like exercising that way. But you need not do any more than walk briskly for 30 minutes a day to obtain most of the benefits of exercise. Some mild weight-lifting exercises are also recommended to keep your muscles and bones strong. Many researchers believe that time invested in doing this level of exercise will be fully paid back in prolonged life. Moreover, a 30-minute brisk walk daily can result in a weight loss of up to 20 pounds in one year without even dieting.

If you have not exercised for some time, please consult your physician before starting an exercise program.

Myths and Facts
Myth: *Exercise increases appetite*
Fact: Moderate exercise actually reduces appetite. Vigorous and extensive exercise increases appetite when the body needs extra calories to make up for the used-up energy.

The Third Pillar - Managing Stress through Balance

"Stress is a relatively new concept in our culture and yet most of us will eventually die of disorders related to our inability to cope successfully with it."

Thomas H. Budzynski, Ph.D.
Quoted from "How to Kill Stress Before It Kills You"
by M. Culligan and K. Sedlacek, M.D.

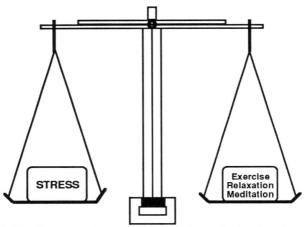

Stress, defined as mental or emotional strain or tension, is ever present and ever increasing in today's modern industrial life. The fast pace of life; the ever increasing demand for higher productivity; a competitive environment; the constant rat-race for advancement; coping with commuting and traffic jams; and concerns about family, health, finances, job security, lack of time, and an endless number of other things can heighten stress to a destructive level. Unless stress can be controlled it can lead to many problems including emotional disorders and physical ones like high blood pressure, raised blood cholesterol level, chest pains and even heart attacks.

There is not much you can do about the stress producing factors that are beyond your control, but you can learn to manage the level of emotional strain and tension you experience. Stress management is now recognized to be an essential part of a heart health regimen along with diet and exercise.

Popular stress reduction techniques include:

- Relaxation and other exercises
- Recreational activities
- Prayer and meditation

It would seem that stresses build up overwhelmingly when life becomes lopsided due to excessive concentration on the material things from which stress per se derives, and that life must be balanced by activities that relieve the mind from such pressures from time to time. Stress control requires people to achieve a balance in their lives between the material and the non-material or spiritual. Eastern philosophies refer to this as establishing harmony with nature and maintain that when one upsets this harmony, one raises the possibility of numerous physical disorders.

A long walk in the park, an absorbing hobby, reminiscing over a pleasant thought, taking a break from routine, giving a little of oneself for the benefit of others, praying or meditating, all help to give tranquility to the mind. Meditation is increasingly used as a discipline by highly pressured corporate executives for stress relief. Its popularity comes not only because it relieves stress, but because it also seems to enrich the spirit, charge up the mind, and increase creativity and efficiency. Dr. Dean Ornish, who has carried out a study on successfully reversing heart disease is a great believer in the therapeutic value of meditation. He defines meditation as ". . . a focusing of the mind for a time on a sound, a word, a prayer -- a way of quieting the mind and body and experiencing inner peace." [Reader's Digest, February, 1991, page 23]. Certain Eastern traditions believe that meditation is a spiritual exercise of much more profound significance.

"The best doctors in the world are Doctor Diet, Doctor Quiet, and Doctor Merryman."

Jonathan Swift
Polite Conversation II (1738)

About Recipes in this Book

There is general agreement that the diets of people in western industrialized countries has a far higher content of fat, saturated fat, cholesterol, sodium and sugar, and a much lower content of fiber than is healthful for them. Therefore, in modifying Indian recipes, my goal was to ensure that the new recipes would have acceptable levels of these nutrients, and that the readers would be able to construct diet plans to meet their individual requirements.

I have used the following principles to modify recipes. Readers of this book may use these same principles to alter their favorite recipes.

Lowering Content of Saturated Fats

- Butter, ghee (clarified butter or butter oil), vegetable ghee, and all oils which have a high content of saturated fats such as coconut and other tropical oils as well as hydrogenated oils (see "Understanding Fats and Oils" on page 246) have been avoided. Instead, I have only used canola oil (except the occasional use of corn or canola margarine in some recipes). Canola oil which is extracted from rapeseed has the lowest saturated fat content of all oils generally available. Other acceptable oils such as corn, safflower, sunflower, soybean and olive oil may be used. However, please note that the nutrient analysis for each recipe is based only on the listed ingredients -- any substitution may alter the analysis.

  Please use only liquid oils from the acceptable oils listed above. Many grocery stores sell bulk canola, corn and other 100% vegetable oils which are hydrogenated. How can you tell? Saturated fats will set in the refrigerator and often even at room temperature: these fats should not be used in your diet.

- Margarine is a good substitute for butter, but you have to be careful:

  First, only use margarines which list liquid canola oil, or one of the acceptable oils, as the first ingredient and partially-hydrogenated [acceptable] oil as the second ingredient on the food label. (Please read "Understanding Food Labels" on page 257).

Second, although acceptable margarines are better than butter because of their lower saturated fat content, there are some indications that they still may tend to raise blood cholesterol. Therefore use margarine in moderation.

- Eat chicken, turkey or fish instead of beef or lamb. With skin and all visible fat removed before cooking, turkey and chicken have a much lower fat content than other meats. However, an occasional indulgence in beef is alright provided that you choose a cut such as very lean sirloin and remove all visible fat before and after cooking. Similarly, a lean cut from a leg of lamb can also be eaten on occasion.

- Substitute ground turkey breast (without skin) instead of ground beef -- you will hardly notice the difference. Please note: store-prepared ground meats tend to have a high fat content; please read the label on the package to verify fat content or ask the butcher in the store.

- Use non-fat or low-fat dairy products such as nonfat milk, yogurt and cheese. If you love ice cream, switch to ice milk, nonfat ice cream, or nonfat frozen yogurt.

Lowering Total Fat Content

- Use less oil in cooking. Fried onions and spices form the base of many Indian dishes. Reducing oil to the bare minimum makes frying onions difficult. Most recipes in this book call for sautéing onions in a small amount of oil, which works well although the process may take longer. In cases where frying is a must, drain and discard excess oil after frying onions. In some recipes I have specified the use of vegetable oil sprays. These sprays, used properly, will allow you to coat a 10-inch nonstick pan or skillet with just one gram or less of oil.

- Cut down on fried foods. Only a few fried-food recipes are included in this book. Although these have acceptable nutrient values as part of an overall diet, they should be consumed only occasionally. Judicious consumption of a variety of foods will alleviate any feeling of deprivation.

- Switch to low-fat or non-fat products. This applies to ingredients and prepared foods that you buy from stores. Understanding food labels (see page 257) helps in avoiding foods with large amounts of fat.

Cutting Down On Cholesterol

- Cholesterol only comes from foods of animal origin.
- Vegetarian dishes, except those that contain milk products, are completely cholesterol free.   Dishes which have milk, yogurt or cheese (Paneer) will have some cholesterol; this is minimized by using non-fat milk products in most cases, and only sometimes low-fat milk products.
- Non-vegetarian dishes, those containing meat or fish, contain cholesterol. By limiting meat or fish to 4 ounces (raw weight) per serving, and to a maximum of two servings per day, cholesterol consumption can be kept within acceptable levels. Meats with high cholesterol content such as brains, liver, heart and kidneys have not been used in any of the recipes. Where meat with bones is an ingredient in any of the recipes in this book, the specified quantity of the ingredient takes into account the non-edible portion (bones).
- Use egg whites instead of whole eggs. Whole eggs have a high cholesterol content. All of the cholesterol is contained in the yolk, which has about 220 milligrams in a large egg -- almost the maximum daily allowance.   Egg whites are nutritious, do not have any cholesterol, and you can eat as many as you like. In most baking recipes you can use two egg whites plus one or two teaspoons of acceptable oil in place of one whole egg.
- Meat, fish and dairy products are a good source of protein. But, you can derive protein from other sources such as lentils which are not only protein rich but also completely free of cholesterol.

Reducing Sodium

- Reduce the amount of salt in cooking. Each teaspoon of salt contains about 2150 milligrams of sodium.
- Sodium is naturally present in almost all food ingredients. The human body normally needs only a few hundred milligrams of sodium per day. If we did not use any salt in our cooking or at the table, the body would probably still get all the sodium it needs naturally.   The general health guidelines recommend a limit of less than 3000 milligrams of sodium intake per day for a healthy adult, and even less for

individuals suffering from high blood pressure. Please see "Understanding Sodium and Salt" on page 251.

- Recipes in this book contain relatively small quantities of salt, use of which is optional. Nutrient analysis for each recipe gives the sodium content with and without added salt. Use of spices, lemon juice and yogurt during cooking and at the table makes up for the reduced saltiness. Human nature being what it is, some readers will be tempted to add more salt than specified in the recipe; should you do so, please remember that each extra teaspoon of salt will add 2150 milligrams of sodium to the recipe. (Please see page 266 for suggestions on painless ways of adjusting to a low-fat, low-salt diet).

Reducing Sugar

- Sugars such as cane and beet sugar, jaggery, honey, etc. are known as simple sugars. These provide only 'empty calories, that is, they provide very few nutrients besides calories. Too much sugar in a diet could have undesirable effects on a person's health, and therefore should be minimized. (Please also read "Understanding Carbohydrates" on page 250).

- Indian cuisine has an abundance of delectable sweets and desserts. The traditional sweet dishes are generally rich in sugar (as well as butter and full cream milk products). These dishes are not included in this book. The sweet dishes that are included are made *with reduced amount of sugar* as well as with nonfat milk products and acceptable vegetable oils.

Increasing Fiber

- Indian food is potentially fiber rich. Most Indians eat vegetables, daals, lentils, peas and beans with Chapati (also known as Rotli or Roti -- an unleavened bread made with whole wheat flour), all of which provide a good amount of fiber. In my Indian bread recipes I have added oat bran, which not only adds to the taste, but also adds insoluble fiber, and soluble fiber which is reputed to assist in reduction of blood cholesterol.

Nutrient Analysis of Recipes

Each recipe has been analyzed for the number of calories, and the amount of protein, carbohydrates, total fat, saturated fat, cholesterol and sodium, based on the listed ingredients. Brief explanations of these nutrients are given later in this book.

All volumetric measures such as cups, tablespoons and teaspoons are *level* measures:

1 cup = 8 fluid ounces (225 ml)
1 tablespoon (tbsp) = 1/2 fluid ounce (15 ml)
1 teaspoon (tsp) = 1/6 fluid ounce (5 ml)
1 pound (lb) = 16 ounces (oz) (455 grams)

Explanation of measures, and conversion tables for metric and imperial measures can be found on page 243 to assist readers in Australia, Bangladesh, Britain, Canada, Europe, India, Pakistan, Sri Lanka and other countries.

A computerized data base comprising of the USDA Survey Data, the USDA Handbook 8, the Canadian Nutrient File and manufacturers' nutrient data was used to calculate food values for each recipe. For the recipes in which foods are deep fried, the actual amount of oil absorbed was measured at the time of testing recipes and included in the analysis.

Adjusting to Taste

It is realized that spiciness of food is a matter of taste. If you like your food more or less spicy, please feel free to adjust the quantities of ground spices and chili powder and the amount of lemon juice (if called for in the recipe). These adjustments will make a negligible difference to the nutrient analysis. However, adjustment of quantities of other ingredients such as oils, fats, salt, sugar, meats, milk products, lentils, rice and vegetables will alter the analysis.

Abbreviations used in this book

tsp = teaspoon	tbsp = tablespoon	ml = milliliter
fl. oz = fluid ounce(s)	oz = ounce(s)	lb(s) = pounds(s)
mg = milligram(s)	gm(s) = gram(s)	kg = kilograms
in = inch(es)	ft = feet	cm = centimeters
w/ = with	w/o = without	tr = trace

Recipes

Soups

Vegetarian

Mung Bean Soup	20
Red Lentil Soup	21
Mixed Vegetable Soup	22
Lentil and Vegetable Soup	23

Non-vegetarian

Fish Soup	24
Hearty Chicken Soup	25
Quick Chicken Soup	26

Please also see:

Plain Daal	104
Daal with Mustard Seeds	106
Kadhi	112

Mung Bean Soup

For 8 servings you will need:

1   cup whole mung beans, sorted, washed and soaked overnight
6   cups water
1   cup onions, finely chopped
1   cup celery, finely chopped
1   cup tomatoes, fresh or canned without salt, blended,
1   teaspoon garlic, minced
1/4   teaspoon ground black pepper
1/4   teaspoon ground turmeric
1/4   cup cilantro, finely chopped
2   tablespoons lemon juice
8   tablespoons nonfat yogurt

To prepare:

1. Drain, rinse and drain mung beans.
2. In a large saucepan, bring drained mung beans and water to boil. Cook for 10 minutes, skimming off any froth that forms.
3. Add onions, celery, tomatoes, garlic, black pepper, turmeric and bring to boil again.
4. Lower heat slightly, cover and cook for 30 minutes. Add more water if necessary.
5. Lower the heat and simmer for 15 minutes or until the mung beans are soft.
6. Add cilantro and lemon juice, mix and remove from heat.
7. Serve in eight individual bowls, each topped with one tablespoon of nonfat yogurt.

Note: This recipe has no salt or oil.

Nutrient Analysis (per serving):

Calories	123
Protein	8.5 gm
Carbohydrates	22.4 gm
Total Fat	0.5 gm
Saturated Fat	0.1 gm
Cholesterol	0.5 mg
Sodium	42.4 mg

Red Lentil Soup

For 8 servings you will need:

1¼   *cup split red lentils (masoor daal)*
1   *tablespoon canola oil*
1   *cup onions, finely diced*
1/2   *cup celery, finely diced*
12   *whole peppercorns*
1   *tablespoon all-purpose flour*
1   *cup carrots, finely diced*
2   *cups tomatoes, fresh or canned without salt, blended*
1/4   *teaspoon ground turmeric*
3/4   *teaspoon salt (optional)*
1   *teaspoon sugar*
6   *cups water*

To prepare:

1. Sort, wash lentils in cold water and drain.
2. In a large saucepan, heat canola oil and sauté onions, celery and whole peppercorns until the onions and celery are soft.
3. Sprinkle flour over the onions and celery and cook for 1 minute. Stir to mix.
4. Add lentils, carrots, tomatoes, turmeric, salt and sugar. Mix well, and cook for 5 minutes, stirring frequently.
5. Add water, stir and let the soup come to boil. Lower the heat slightly, cover, and cook for 40 minutes or until lentils are soft.
6. Whisk or blend until smooth and serve.

Please discard whole peppercorns when eating.

Nutrient Analysis (per serving):

Calories	150
Protein	9.4 gm
Carbohydrates	24.7 gm
Total Fat	2.3 gm
Saturated Fat	0.2 gm
Cholesterol	0 mg
Sodium with salt included	218.9 mg
Sodium with salt omitted	17.3 mg

Mixed Vegetable Soup

For 10 servings you will need:

1   tablespoon canola oil
1   cup onions, finely diced
1   cup celery, finely diced
20   whole black peppercorns
1   tablespoon all-purpose flour
2   cups tomatoes, fresh or canned without salt, blended
1/2 teaspoon salt (optional)
1/4 teaspoon ground turmeric
1   cup carrots, diced
1   cup peas
1   cup cabbage, shredded
1   cup potatoes, peeled and diced
6   cups water
2   tablespoons lemon juice

To prepare:

1. In a large saucepan, heat oil and sauté onions, celery and whole black peppercorns until the onions and celery are soft.
2. Sprinkle flour over onion and celery and cook for 1 minute. Stir to mix.
3. Add tomatoes, salt and turmeric, mix well, and cook for 5 minutes.
4. Add the remaining vegetables and water, stir and bring to boil. Reduce heat to a slow boiling point and cook for 30 minutes, or until the vegetables are cooked. If soup is too thick, add some water.
5. Add lemon juice, mix and serve.

Please discard whole black peppercorns when eating, .

Nutrient Analysis (per serving):

Calories	71
Protein	2.3 gm
Carbohydrates	12.7 gm
Total Fat	1.7 gm
Saturated Fat	0.2 gm
Cholesterol	0 mg
Sodium with salt included	128.4 mg
Sodium with salt omitted	21.8 mg

Lentil and Vegetable Soup

For 10 servings you will need:

1   *cup masoor daal (split red lentils)*
7   *cups water*
1   *cup onions, finely diced*
1   *cup celery, diced*
1   *cup potatoes, diced*
1   *cup carrots, diced*
1   *cup peas*
1   *cup cabbage, shredded*
1   *cup green beans, cut into pieces*
2   *cups tomatoes, fresh or canned without salt, blended*
1/4 *teaspoon ground turmeric*
1/2 *teaspoon salt (optional)*
20   *whole black peppercorns*
2   *tablespoons lemon juice*

To prepare:

1. Sort, wash lentils in cold water and drain.
2. In a large saucepan, bring to boil water, lentils and all remaining ingredients except lemon juice.
3. Reduce heat slightly, cover and cook for 1 hour or until the lentils and vegetables are tender. If soup is too thick, add some water.
4. Add lemon juice, mix and serve.

Please discard whole peppercorns when eating.

Note: This recipe has no oil.

Nutrient Analysis (per serving):

Calories	112
Protein	7.4 gm
Carbohydrates	21.3 gm
Total Fat	0.4 gm
Saturated Fat	0.1 gm
Cholesterol	0 mg
Sodium with salt included	129.2 mg
Sodium with salt omitted	21.7 mg

Fish Soup

For 4 servings you will need:

1	cup onion, finely diced
1/2	cup celery, finely diced
2	1-inch sticks cinnamon
10	whole black peppercorns
3	teaspoons garlic, minced
3	teaspoons root ginger, minced
1/4	teaspoon ground turmeric
2	cups tomatoes, fresh or canned without salt, blended
1/4	teaspoon salt (optional)
1	pound halibut,* (approx. 4 ounces per serving), cleaned and cubed
6	cups water
1/2	pound potatoes, peeled and cubed
1/2	cup cilantro, finely chopped
2	tablespoons lemon juice

To prepare:

1. In a large saucepan, bring to boil all the ingredients except potatoes, cilantro and lemon juice.
2. Reduce heat slightly, cover and cook for 15 minutes.
3. Add potatoes and cilantro, mix well, cover and cook for 15 minutes, or until the potatoes are done.
4. Add lemon juice and serve.

Please discard whole spices when eating.

* Other white fish may be substituted for halibut.

Nutrient Analysis (per serving):

Calories	172
Protein	21.2 gm
Carbohydrates	22.8 gm
Total Fat	2.5 gm
Saturated Fat	0.4 gm
Cholesterol	29.0 mg
Sodium with salt included	186.0 mg
Sodium with salt omitted	78.0 mg

Hearty Chicken Soup

For 6 servings you will need:

1   *tablespoon canola oil*
1   *cup onion, finely diced*
1/2   *cup celery, finely diced*
2   *1-inch cinnamon sticks*
12   *whole black peppercorns*
1¼   *pound chicken breasts, (approx 3½ ounces per serving),*
      skinned, all visible fat removed and cut into pieces
3   *teaspoons garlic, minced*
3   *teaspoons root ginger, minced*
1/4   *teaspoon salt (optional)*
1/4   *teaspoon ground turmeric*
2   *cups tomatoes, fresh or canned without salt, blended*
6   *cups water*
1/2   *pound potatoes, peeled and cut into 12 pieces*
1/2   *cup cilantro, chopped*
2   *tablespoons lemon juice*

To prepare:

1. In a saucepan, heat oil and sauté onions, celery, cinnamon and peppercorns until onions and celery are soft. Do not let onions brown.
2. Add chicken, garlic, ginger, salt, turmeric and tomatoes. Mix well, cover and cook for 15 minutes. Stir occasionally.
3. Add 6 cups of water, potatoes and cilantro. Mix well, cover and cook for 15 minutes or until the potatoes are done.
4. Add lemon juice. mix and serve.

Please discard whole spices while eating.

Nutrient Analysis (per serving):

Calories	167
Protein	19.5 gm
Carbohydrates	14.5 gm
Total Fat	3.6 gm
Saturated Fat	0.5 gm
Cholesterol	43.9 mg
Sodium with salt included	156.6 mg
Sodium with salt omitted	66.3 mg

Quick Chicken Soup

For 6 servings you will need:

1¼ pounds chicken breasts, (approx 3½ ounces per serving), skinned, all visible fat removed and cut into pieces
3   teaspoons garlic, minced
3   teaspoons ginger, minced
1/4 teaspoon salt (optional)
1/4 teaspoon ground turmeric
1   cup onions, finely chopped
1/2 cup celery, finely chopped
2   1-inch sticks cinnamon
2   whole cloves
12 whole black peppercorns
6   cups water
2   tablespoons lemon juice
1/4 cup cilantro, finely chopped

To prepare:

1. In a large saucepan, bring to boil all the ingredients except cilantro and lemon juice.
2. Reduce heat to a slow boiling point, cover, and cook for 45 minutes.
3. Add lemon juice, mix, garnish with cilantro and serve.

Please discard whole spices when eating.

Nutrient Analysis (per serving):

Calories	101
Protein	18.1 gm
Carbohydrates	4.1 gm
Total Fat	1.1 gm
Saturated Fat	0.3 gm
Cholesterol	43.9 mg
Sodium with salt included	148.5 mg
Sodium with salt omitted	58.7 mg

Savory Snacks and Starters

For Sweet Starters see Desserts and Sweets on page 181

Steamed Savory Cake
Dhokra

For 1 cake (8 servings) you will need:

Ingredients for the batter:
1   *cup cream of wheat*
1/2 *cup gram flour (chickpea flour)*
1   *cup low fat yogurt*
1   *cup water*
1   *teaspoon garlic, minced*
1   *teaspoon root ginger, minced*
1   *green chili, seeded and minced*
1/4 *cup cilantro, finely chopped*
1   *teaspoon ground cumin*
1/8 *teaspoon ground turmeric*
1/2 *teaspoon salt (optional)*
1   *tablespoon lemon juice*
3/4 *tablespoon canola oil (for the batter)*

1/2 *teaspoon canola oil (for coating the cake pan)*
1   *teaspoon Eno's Fruit Salt (see page 240)*
16   *whole black peppercorns*

To prepare:

1. In a large bowl, combine all the batter ingredients into a
    smooth mixture.
2. Prepare a steamer capable of holding a 9-inch round, 1½inch
    deep cake pan.
3. Coat a 9-inch non-stick cake pan with 1/2 teaspoon of oil.
4. Add Eno's Fruit Salt to the batter and mix well. Immediately
    pour the batter into the prepared cake pan and sprinkle whole
    peppercorns on top.
5. Place the cake pan in the steamer, cover, and steam for 15 to
    20 minutes. Test with a wooden toothpick. Remove from
    steamer when the toothpick comes out clean.
6. Allow Dhokra to cool, turn out onto a plate, and cut into 8
    slices.

Steamed Savory Cake
Dhokra

Serve hot or cold with Salads, Pickles, Chutneys and Raita of your choice (page 61).

Nutrient Analysis (per serving):

Calories	184
Protein	6.8 gm
Carbohydrates	26.3 gm
Total Fat	5.9 gm
Saturated Fat	1.1 gm
Cholesterol	1.7 mg
Sodium with salt included	235.2 mg
Sodium with salt omitted	101.4 mg

Savory Lentil and Vegetable Cake
Andhvo

For 1 cake (8 servings) you will need:

```
-------------------------------------------
```
Ingredients for the batter:
1   *cup cream of wheat*
1/2 *cup gram flour (chickpea flour)*
1   *cup low fat plain yogurt*
1   *cup water*
2   *teaspoons garlic, minced*
2   *teaspoons root ginger, minced*
1   *green chilli, seeded and minced*
1/4 *cup cilantro, finely chopped*
1/4 *teaspoon ground turmeric*
1/2 *teaspoon salt (optional)*
2   *tablespoons lemon juice*
```
-------------------------------------------
```
1/2 *cup onion, finely diced*
1/2 *cup potato, peeled and grated*
1/3 *cup carrots, peeled and grated*
1/2 *cup peas*
5   *teaspoons canola oil*
1/2 *tablespoon whole black mustard seeds*
1   *teaspoon cumin seeds*
1   *tablespoon sesame seeds*
4   *curry leaves, broken*
1   *teaspoon Eno's Fruit Salt (see page 240)*

To prepare:

1. Preheat oven to 400° F.
2. In a large bowl, combine all the batter ingredients into a smooth mixture.
3. Add onions, potatoes, carrots and peas to the batter, and mix well.

Savory Lentil and Vegetable Cake
Andhvo

4. In a small saucepan, heat 4 teaspoons oil and fry mustard seeds, cumin seeds and curry leaves until seeds begin to splutter, about 15 seconds. Immediately pour into the batter and mix well.
5. Prepare a 9-inch non-stick cake pan: coat the base with 1 teaspoon oil, sprinkle 1 tablespoon sesame seeds evenly over the base, and roast in the preheated oven for 3 minutes. Remove.
6. Add Eno's Fruit Salt to the batter, mix well and immediately pour into the prepared cake pan. Bake in the preheated oven for 30 to 45 minutes.
7. Test with a wooden toothpick. Remove Andhvo from the oven when the toothpick comes away clean.
8. Allow Andhvo to cool, turn out onto a plate, and cut into 8 slices.

Serve hot or cold with Salads, Pickles, Chutneys and Raita of your choice (page 61).

Nutrient Analysis (per serving):

Calories	202
Protein	8.1 gm
Carbohydrates	31.2 gm
Total Fat	5.3 gm
Saturated Fat	0.7 gm
Cholesterol	1.7 mg
Sodium with salt included	238.3 mg
Sodium with salt omitted	104.6 mg

Spinach Cake

For 1 cake (25 squares) you will need:

2   cups gram flour (chickpea flour)
1/2   teaspoon baking powder
3/4   teaspoon salt (optional)
2   teaspoons ground cumin
1/4   teaspoon ground turmeric
1/4   teaspoon red chili powder (optional)
2   teaspoons garlic, minced
1-2   green chilies, seeded and minced
1   teaspoon ajma (omum) seeds
1   cup tamarind sauce (see page 227)
1/2   cup nonfat yogurt
2   tablespoons canola oil
3   cups tightly packed washed and chopped spinach
1/4   cup cilantro, finely chopped
     vegetable oil spray
1   clove garlic, sliced
1/2   teaspoon black mustard seeds
2   teaspoons sesame seeds
4   curry leaves, broken

To prepare:

1. Preheat oven to 350° F.
2. In a bowl, combine sifted gram flour, baking powder, salt, cumin, turmeric, chili powder, garlic, green chilies and ajma.
3. Gradually add Tamarind Sauce and nonfat yogurt and make a smooth batter.
4. Add 1 tablespoon oil and mix well. Fold in spinach and cilantro.
5. Spray an 8-inch square nonstick baking pan with vegetable oil spray, pour in the batter, cover with foil and bake in the preheated oven for 1 hour. Test with a wooden toothpick; remove cake from the oven when the toothpick comes away clean.
6. When cool, turn out the cake onto a plate and cut into 25 squares.

Spinach Cake

7. In a saucepan, heat 1 tablespoon canola oil and fry sliced garlic for 15 seconds.
8. Add mustard seeds, sesame seeds and curry leaves and fry for 15 seconds or until the seeds begin to splutter. Remove from heat and immediately add the Spinach Cake squares, toss and carefully turn with a spoon so as to distribute the seeds evenly over the Spinach Cake squares.
9. Return saucepan to heat, add 2 tablespoons of water, reduce heat, cover and cook for about 5 minutes, or until heated through.

Serve hot or cold with Salads, Pickles, Chutneys and Raita of your choice (page 61).

Nutrient Analysis (per square):

Calories	82
Protein	3.8 gm
Carbohydrates	12.1 gm
Total Fat	2.4 gm
Saturated Fat	0.2 gm
Cholesterol	0.1 mg
Sodium with salt included	86.54 mg
Sodium with salt omitted	21.8 mg

Lentil Fritters in Yogurt
Dahi Vada

For 16 servings you will need:

For Fritters (Vada):
1/2 cup mung daal (hulled and split mung beans)
1/2 cup urad daal (hulled and split black mung)
1/2 teaspoon baking powder, low sodium
2   teaspoons garlic, minced
2   teaspoons root ginger, minced
1-2 green chilies, minced
1/2 cup cilantro, finely chopped
1/2 teaspoon ground cumin
1/4 teaspoon salt (optional)
     canola oil for frying

For Yogurt Sauce:
2   cups nonfat yogurt
1   teaspoon sugar
1   teaspoon cumin seeds, coarsely ground
1   green chili, finely chopped
1   dash ground black pepper

For Garnish:
1/4 teaspoon red chili powder (optional)
1/4 cup cilantro, finely chopped

To prepare:

1. Sort, wash and soak, in separate bowls, mung and urad daals in water for 5 hours or overnight.
2. Drain and blend both daals into a near smooth mixture and pour into a bowl. Add a little water if necessary.
3. Add baking powder, garlic, ginger, green chilies, cilantro, cumin and salt. Mix well.
4. To make Yogurt Sauce, in a jug, mix yogurt, sugar, cumin seeds, green chili and black pepper. Set aside.
5. Fill a saucepan with ice-cold water and set aside.

Lentil Fritters in Yogurt
Dahi Vada

6. In a deep frying pan, heat oil. Divide lentil mixture into 16 portions (about 2 tablespoons each). With moist hands, shape each portion into a round ball, flatten slightly and deep fry Vada, turning frequently, until golden.
7. Lift Vada with a slotted spoon and drop into the ice-cold water. Allow to soak for 10 to15 minutes.
8. Lift out each Vada, squeeze out excess water by pressing between palms of you hands and arrange in a deep serving dish.
9. Pour Yogurt Sauce over the Vada. Garnish with red chili powder and cilantro before serving.

Serve with Salads, Chutneys and Pickles of your choice (page 61).

Author's Note: Deep-fried foods are recommended for occasional eating only, even though they are made of healthful ingredients.

Nutrient Analysis (per serving):

Calories	80
Protein	4.8 gm
Carbohydrates	11.1 gm
Total Fat	2.0 gm
Saturated Fat	0.2 gm
Cholesterol	0.5 mg
Sodium with salt included	57.6 mg
Sodium with salt omitted	24.0 mg

Mung Cutlets

For 16 cutlets you will need:

1¼ cups husked mung daal, sorted, washed and soaked overnight
1   cup peas
1/4 cup carrots, chopped
2   green chilies
1/2 cup cilantro
2   teaspoons garlic, minced
2   teaspoons root ginger, minced
1/4 teaspoon red chili powder
1/4 teaspoon ground turmeric
3   teaspoons ground cumin
3/4 teaspoon salt (optional)
1   cup onions, finely diced
2   tablespoons lemon juice
     vegetable oil spray

To prepare:

1. Drain and blend mung daal into a coarse mixture and pour into a bowl.
2. Blend peas, carrots, green chilies and cilantro into a coarse mixture and add to the blended mung daal. Add remaining ingredients except vegetable oil spray and mix well.
3. Spray a nonstick frying pan lightly with vegetable oil spray. Drop about 2 tablespoonfuls of mixture onto the frying pan and spread into a 3 to 3½ inch round cutlet with the back of a spoon. Make as many cutlets as the pan will hold.
4. Cook each side until mottled brown, turning over once.
5   Repeat steps 3 and 4 for the remaining mixture. Makes 16.
Serve hot or cold on their own or in Naan pockets with Salads, Pickles, Chutneys and Raita of your choice (page 61).

Nutrient Analysis (per cutlet):

Calories	71
Protein	4.5 gm
Carbohydrates	12.8 gm
Total Fat	0.6 gm
Saturated Fat	0.1 gm
Cholesterol	0 mg
Sodium with salt included	104.8 mg
Sodium with salt omitted	4.2 mg

Mung Fritters
Mung Vada

For 24 fritters you will need:

1½   *cups husked mung daal, sorted, washed and soaked overnight*
2   *teaspoons garlic, minced*
2   *teaspoons ginger, minced*
1-2 *green chilies, finely chopped*
1/4   *teaspoon red chili powder (optional)*
1/4   *teaspoon ground turmeric*
3   *teaspoons ground cumin*
1/4   *teaspoon citric acid*
1/2   *teaspoon salt (optional)*
1   *cup onions or spring onions, finely diced*
2   *tablespoons lemon juice*
     canola oil for deep frying

To prepare:

1. Drain and blend mung daal into a coarse mixture. Pour the mixture into a bowl.
2. Add all the remaining ingredients except oil, and mix well.
3. In a deep frying pan, heat oil . Carefully drop about 2-tablespoonful measures of the mixture into the hot oil and fry, turning frequently, until golden brown. Lift with a slotted spoon and drain in a colander lined with paper towels.

Serve hot or cold with Salads, Pickles, Chutneys and Raita of your choice (page 61).

Author's Note: Deep-fried foods are recommended for occasional eating only, even though they are made of healthful ingredients.

Nutrient Analysis (per fritter):

Calories	69
Protein	4.1 gm
Carbohydrates	9.7 gm
Total Fat	1.8 gm
Saturated Fat	0.1 gm
Cholesterol	0 mg
Sodium with salt included	48.1 mg
Sodium with salt omitted	2.6 mg

Savory Fritters
Pakora

For 24 Pakoras you will need:

1	cup gram (chickpea) flour
1/2	teaspoon baking powder (low sodium)
1/2	cup water (approximately)
2	teaspoons garlic, minced
1/4	teaspoon salt (optional)
1	teaspoon whole cumin, coarsely crushed
2	teaspoons ground coriander
1/4	teaspoon ground turmeric
1/4	teaspoon red chili powder (optional)
1/4	teaspoon ajma (omum) seeds
1	green chili, seeded and finely chopped (optional)
1	cup onions, peeled and finely diced
1	cup potatoes, peeled and cut into thin round slices
1/4	cup cilantro, chopped
1	teaspoon canola oil, for the batter
	canola oil for frying

To prepare:

1. In a bowl, combine sifted gram flour and baking powder. Gradually add water and make a smooth batter. Let stand for 15 minutes.
2. Add garlic, salt, cumin, coriander, turmeric, chili powder, green chili and ajma, and mix thoroughly.
3. Add onions, potatoes, cilantro and 1 teaspoon canola oil and mix well.
4. In a deep frying pan, heat oil. Take spoonfuls of batter, each with one potato slice, and carefully drop into the hot oil. (Do not overcrowd the pan; fry just enough to cover the surface of the oil). Fry, turning frequently, until Pakoras are crisp and deep gold in color. Remove and drain in a colander lined with paper towels.

Serve hot or cold with Salads, Pickles, Chutneys and Raita of your choice (page 61).

Savory Fritters
Pakora

Variations: Instead of potatoes use one or more of the following vegetables: onion rings, mild green chilies (slit), bell pepper rings, sliced eggplant, sliced zucchini, cauliflower florets, broccoli florets or chopped spinach.

Pakora are also known as Bhajya

Author's Note: Deep-fried foods are recommended for occasional eating only, even though they are made of healthful ingredients.

Nutrient Analysis (per Pakora):

Calories	57
Protein	1.9 gm
Carbohydrates	7.2 gm
Total Fat	2.5 gm
Saturated Fat	0.2 gm
Cholesterol	0 mg
Sodium with salt included	25.2 mg
Sodium with salt omitted	2.8 mg

Chickpeas and Potato Salad
Chana Bateta

For 6 servings you will need:

1   cup dark brown chickpeas, sorted, washed and soaked overnight*
3/4   pound potatoes
2   cups Tamarind Sauce (see page 227)
1   cup water
2   teaspoons canola oil
1/2   teaspoon black mustard seeds
1   green chili, seeded and chopped
1/4   teaspoon ground turmeric
1/2   teaspoon salt (optional)
1/4   teaspoon red chili powder
2   teaspoons sugar
1   tablespoon lemon juice
1/4   cup cilantro, finely chopped

To prepare:

1.   Drain and wash chickpeas thoroughly. In a large saucepan, boil chickpeas in water for 50 minutes or until soft. Drain.
2.   Boil unpeeled potatoes until cooked. When cool, peel and cut into about 1/2-inch cubes. Set aside.
3.   In a large saucepan, heat oil and fry mustard seeds until the seeds begin to splutter; about 15 seconds.
4.   Add green chilies, turmeric and salt. Cook for 10 seconds and immediately add Tamarind Sauce, water, drained chickpeas, chili powder and sugar, and bring to boil.
5.   Reduce heat, cover and simmer for 10 minutes. Add a little water if too dry.
6.   Add three-quarters of the potato cubes into the saucepan. Mash the remaining potatoes and add to the saucepan. Stir, cover and cook for 10 minutes.
7.   Add lemon juice and cilantro. Mix and serve.

Serve hot or cold with savory snacks or as a side dish.

* Note: Drained, low-salt canned Garbanzo beans may be used instead, omitting Step 1.

Chickpeas and Potato Salad
Chana Bateta

Nutrient Analysis (per serving):

Calories	213
Protein	8.1 gm
Carbohydrates	38.8 gm
Total Fat	3.8 gm
Saturated Fat	0.4 gm
Cholesterol	0 mg
Sodium with salt included	240.3 mg
Sodium with salt omitted	61.1 mg

Exotic Vegetable Triangles
Vegetable Samosa

To make 24 you will need:

1/2 tablespoon canola oil
1/2 teaspoon black mustard seeds
5 curry leaves, broken
1 cup peas
1 cup green beans, finely chopped
1 cup carrots, finely diced
1½ cups potatoes, peeled, cut into 1/4 inch cubes
2 teaspoons garlic, minced
2 teaspoons root ginger, minced
3/4 teaspoon salt (optional)
2 teaspoons ground cumin
1/2 teaspoon ground turmeric
1/2 teaspoon red chili powder (optional)
1 tablespoon lemon juice
1/2 cup onions, finely diced
1-2 green chilies, seeded and finely chopped
1/2 cup cilantro, finely chopped
2 teaspoons garam masala
1 recipe Samosa Pastry (see page 230)
  canola oil for frying or vegetable oil spray for baking

To prepare filling:

1. In a saucepan, heat 1/2 tablespoon oil and fry mustard seeds and curry leaves. When the mustard seeds begin to splutter, add peas, green beans, carrots, potatoes, garlic, ginger and salt and mix. Reduce heat slightly, cover and cook for 5 to 7 minutes, stirring occasionally.
2. Add cumin, turmeric, red chili powder and lemon juice and mix. Cook, stirring frequently, for 5 to 7 minutes or until all the liquid has evaporated. Remove from heat.
3. When cool, add onions, green chilies, cilantro and garam masala. Mix well and set aside.

Exotic Vegetable Triangles
Vegetable Samosa

To make Samosa:

1. Follow instructions for folding and filling Samosa on page 232. Then follow either Step 2 **or** Step 3 below.
2. In a deep frying pan, heat oil and deep fry triangles (Samosa) slowly, turning frequently, until golden. Remove with a slotted spoon and drain in a colander lined with paper towels.

- OR -

3. Preheat oven to 400° F. Place Samosa on a baking tray and spray lightly with vegetable oil spray. Turn over the Samosa and again spray lightly with vegetable oil spray. Bake in the preheated oven for 10 to 15 minutes, or until golden, turning once.

Serve hot or cold with Salads, Pickles, Chutneys and Raita of your choice (page 61).

Author's Note: Deep-fried foods are recommended for occasional eating only, even though they are made of healthful ingredients.

Nutrient Analysis (per fried Samosa):

Calories	70
Protein	1.6 gm
Carbohydrates	10.7 gm
Total Fat	2.5 gm
Saturated Fat	0.2 gm
Cholesterol	0 mg
Sodium with salt included	71.2 mg
Sodium with salt omitted	4.0 mg

Nutrient Analysis (per baked Samosa):

Calories	58
Protein	1.6 gm
Carbohydrates	10.7 gm
Total Fat	1.2 gm
Saturated Fat	0.1 gm
Cholesterol	0 mg
Sodium with salt included	71.2 mg
Sodium with salt omitted	4.0 mg

Boiled Turkey Kabab

For 20 Kababs (5 servings) you will need:

1   *pound ground breast of turkey (meat only)*
2   *teaspoons garlic, minced*
2   *teaspoons root ginger, minced*
1   *teaspoon green chilies, seeded and minced*
1/2   *cup cilantro, finely chopped*
3/4   *cup onions, finely chopped*
1/4   *teaspoon salt (optional)*
2   *teaspoons ground coriander*
2   *teaspoons ground cumin*
1/2   *teaspoon garam masala*
1/8   *teaspoon ground turmeric*
2   *tablespoons lemon juice*
4   *cups water (for boiling Kababs)*

To prepare:

1. In a bowl, combine and mix all the ingredients except water. Divide and shape mixture into 20 balls (Kababs).
2. In a saucepan, bring water to boil.
3. Gently drop10 Kababs into the boiling water, one at a time. After water starts boiling again, cook for 10-15 minutes until Kababs are firm. Remove Kababs and place on a plate.
4. Repeat step 3 for the remaining Kababs. Reserve the stock.*

Serve hot or cold with Salads, Pickles and Chutneys of your choice (page 61).
* The stock is used for making Kabab Curry (see page 140).

Nutrient Analysis (per serving):

Calories	120
Protein	23.0 gm
Carbohydrates	4.3 gm
Total Fat	0.9gm
Saturated Fat	0.2 gm
Cholesterol	56.3 mg
Sodium with salt included	154.1 mg
Sodium with salt omitted	47.4 mg

Fried Turkey Kabab

For 20 Kababs you will need:

1   *pound ground breast of turkey (meat only)*
1/2 *cup whole wheat flour*
2   *teaspoons garlic, minced*
2   *teaspoons root ginger, minced*
1   *teaspoon green chilies, seeded and minced*
1/4 *cup cilantro, finely chopped*
1   *cup onions, finely chopped*
1/4 *teaspoon salt (optional)*
2   *teaspoons ground coriander*
2   *teaspoons ground cumin*
1/2 *teaspoon garam masala*
1/4 *teaspoon ground turmeric*
2   *tablespoons lemon juice*
     canola oil for frying

To prepare:

1.   In a bowl, combine and mix all the ingredients except oil.
     Divide and shape the mixture into 20 balls (Kababs).
2.   In a deep frying pan, heat oil and deep fry Kababs, turning
     occasionally, until golden brown. Drain in a colander lined
     with paper towels.

Serve hot or cold with Salads, Pickles, Chutneys and Raita of your
choice (page 61).

Author's Note: Deep-fried foods are recommended for occasional
eating only, even though they are made of healthful ingredients.

Nutrient Analysis (per Kabab):

Calories	53
Protein	6.2 gm
Carbohydrates	3.3 gm
Total Fat	1.7 gm
Saturated Fat	0.2 gm
Cholesterol	14.1 mg
Sodium with salt included	38.9 mg
Sodium with salt omitted	12.0 mg

Potato and Meat Patties
Aloo Kheema Vada

For 24 Vada (Patties) you will need:

1   *pound ground breast of turkey (meat only)*
4   *teaspoons garlic, minced*
4   *teaspoons root ginger, minced*
3   *tablespoons lemon juice*
2   *green chilies, seeded and finely chopped*
3/4 *teaspoon salt (optional)*
4   *teaspoons ground coriander*
4   *teaspoons ground cumin*
1½   *teaspoons garam masala*
1/4 *teaspoon red chili powder (optional)*
1½   *cups onion, finely diced*
1/2 *cup cilantro, finely chopped*
1   *pound potatoes, boiled, skinned and mashed*
3   *egg whites, beaten*
     ground black pepper to taste
1/2 *cup cream of wheat*
     vegetable oil spray

To prepare:

1. In a saucepan, cook turkey, garlic, ginger, lemon juice, green chili and salt on medium heat, stirring continuously and breaking up lumps, until all the liquid has evaporated and the meat is just cooked.
2. Add ground coriander, cumin, garam masala and red chili powder, and mix well. Cook for 5 minutes, stirring frequently, until spices are blended in. Remove from heat.
3. When cool, add onions, cilantro, mashed potatoes and mix thoroughly.
4. Preheat oven to 450° F.
5. Spray a non-stick baking tray with vegetable oil spray.
6. Divide the turkey mixture into 24 portions and shape into round patties. Dip the patties in the beaten egg whites, coat with cream of wheat and place on the prepared baking tray.

Potato and Meat Patties
Aloo Kheema Vada

7. Spray patties lightly with vegetable oil spray and cook in the preheated oven for 20 to 25 minutes, or until the Vada are crisp on the outside.

Serve with Salads, Pickles, Chutneys and Raita of your choice (page 61).

Nutrient Analysis (per Vada):

Calories	54
Protein	6.0 gm
Carbohydrates	6.4 gm
Total Fat	0.5 gm
Saturated Fat	0.1 gm
Cholesterol	11.7 mg
Sodium with salt included	85.0 mg
Sodium with salt omitted	17.8 mg

Exotic Turkey Triangles
Turkey Samosa

To make 24 you will need:

1	*pound ground breast of turkey (meat only)*
4	*teaspoons garlic, minced*
4	*teaspoons root ginger, minced*
2	*tablespoons lemon juice*
1	*green chili, seeded and finely chopped*
1/2	*teaspoon salt (optional)*
2	*teaspoons ground coriander*
2	*teaspoons ground cumin*
1/4	*teaspoon red chili powder (optional)*
1	*teaspoon garam masala*
1½	*cups onions, finely diced*
1/2	*cup cilantro, finely chopped*
1	*recipe Samosa Pastry (see page 230)*
	canola oil for frying or vegetable oil spray for baking

To prepare filling:

1. In a saucepan, cook turkey, garlic, ginger, lemon juice, green chili and salt on medium heat, stirring continuously and breaking up lumps, until all the liquid has evaporated and the meat is just cooked.
2. Add ground coriander, cumin, garam masala and mix well. Cook for 5 minutes, stirring frequently, until spices are blended in. Remove from heat.
3. When cool, add onions and cilantro. Mix well and set aside.

Exotic Turkey Triangles
Turkey Samosa

To make Samosa:

1. Follow instructions for folding and filling Samosa on page 232. Then follow either Step 2 **or** Step 3 below.
2. In a deep frying pan, heat oil and deep fry triangles (Samosa) slowly, turning frequently, until golden. Remove with a slotted spoon and drain in a colander lined with paper towels.

- OR -

3. Preheat oven to 400° F. Place Samosa on a baking tray and spray lightly with vegetable oil spray. Turn over the Samosa and again spray lightly with vegetable oil spray. Bake in the preheated oven for 10 to 15 minutes, or until golden, turning once.

Serve hot or cold with Salads, Pickles, Chutneys and Raita of your choice (page 61).

Author's Note: Deep-fried foods are recommended for occasional eating only, even though they are made of healthful ingredients.

Nutrient Analysis (per fried Samosa):

Calories	73
Protein	5.7 gm
Carbohydrates	7.3 gm
Total Fat	2.3 gm
Saturated Fat	0.2 gm
Cholesterol	11.7 mg
Sodium with salt included	54.9 mg
Sodium with salt omitted	10.0 mg

Nutrient Analysis (per baked Samosa):

Calories	61
Protein	5.7 gm
Carbohydrates	7.3 gm
Total Fat	1.0 gm
Saturated Fat	0.1 gm
Cholesterol	11.7 mg
Sodium with salt included	54.9 mg
Sodium with salt omitted	10.0 mg

Broiled Turkey Kabab
Seekh Kabab

For 20 Kababs you will need:

1   *pound ground breast of turkey (meat only)*
1/2 *cup whole wheat flour*
2   *teaspoons garlic, minced*
2   *teaspoons root ginger, minced*
1   *teaspoon green chilies, seeded and minced*
1/4 *cup cilantro, finely chopped*
1   *cup onions, finely chopped*
1/4 *teaspoon salt (optional)*
2   *teaspoons ground coriander*
2   *teaspoons ground cumin*
1/2 *teaspoon garam masala*
1/4 *teaspoon ground turmeric*
2   *tablespoons lemon juice*

To prepare:

1. Preheat broiler.
2. In a bowl, combine and mix all the ingredients, divide mixture into 20 portions and form into sausage shaped Kababs.
3. Place Kababs on a foil-lined broiler pan and broil, turning occasionally, until light brown and cooked through.

Serve with Peas Pilav (page 100) or Saffron Rice (page 166), and Salad, Pickles, Chutneys and Raita of your choice (page 61).

Nutrient Analysis (per Kabab):

Calories	41
Protein	6.2 gm
Carbohydrates	3.3 gm
Total Fat	0.3 gm
Saturated Fat	0.1 gm
Cholesterol	14.1 mg
Sodium with salt included	38.8 mg
Sodium with salt omitted	8.9 mg

Marinated and Barbecued Chicken Cubes
Chicken Boti Kabab

For 4 servings you will need:

2   *teaspoons garlic, minced*
2   *teaspoons root ginger, minced*
1   *green chili, seeded and minced*
1/4 *cup cilantro, minced*
1/4 *teaspoon salt (optional)*
1/4 *teaspoon red chili powder (optional)*
1/2 *teaspoon garam masala*
1   *teaspoon canola oil*
2   *tablespoons lemon juice*
1   *pound chicken breasts, without skin and bones, cut into 1-inch cubes (approx. 4 ounces per serving)*

To prepare:

1. In a large bowl, combine all the ingredients. Allow the chicken to marinate for 4 to 5 hours or overnight in the refrigerator.
2. Thread chicken cubes onto 4 skewers and broil or barbecue for 5 to 10 minutes, or until cooked, turning as required.

Serve with Naan (pages 174, 176) and/or Saffron Rice (page 166) accompanied by Mixed Vegetables in Sweet and Sour Sauce (page 82), Salads, Pickles, Chutneys and Raita of your choice (page 61).

Author's Note: This dish is also known as Chicken Muskaki.

Nutrient Analysis (per serving):

Calories	146
Protein	26.6 gm
Carbohydrates	2.6 gm
Total Fat	2.7 gm
Saturated Fat	0.5 gm
Cholesterol	65.8 mg
Sodium with salt included	208.9 mg
Sodium with salt omitted	75.2 mg

Exotic Chicken Triangles
Chicken Samosa

To make 24 you will need:

1   *pound ground breast of chicken (meat only)*
4   *teaspoons garlic, minced*
4   *teaspoons root ginger, minced*
1/2 *teaspoon salt (optional)*
2   *tablespoons lemon juice*
1   *green chili, seeded and finely chopped*
2   *teaspoons ground coriander*
2   *teaspoons ground cumin*
1   *teaspoon garam masala*
1/4 *teaspoon red chili powder (optional)*
1½   *cups onions, finely diced*
1/2 *cup cilantro, finely chopped*
1   *recipe Samosa Pastry (see page 230)*
     canola oil for frying or vegetable oil spray for baking

To prepare filling:

1. In a saucepan, cook chicken, garlic, ginger, salt, lemon juice
    and green chili on medium heat, stirring and breaking up
    lumps, until all the liquid has evaporated.
2. Add ground coriander, cumin, garam masala and mix well.
    Cook for 5 to 7 minutes, stirring frequently, until spices are
    blended in.
3. When cool, add onions and cilantro. Mix well and set aside.

Exotic Chicken Triangles
Chicken Samosa

To make Samosa:

1. Follow instructions for folding and filling Samosa on page 232. Then follow either Step 2 or Step 3 below.
2. In a deep frying pan, heat oil and deep fry triangles (Samosa) slowly, turning frequently, until golden. Remove with a slotted spoon and drain in a colander lined with paper towels.

- OR -

3. Preheat oven to 400° F. Place Samosa on a baking tray and spray lightly with vegetable oil spray. Turn over the Samosa and again spray lightly with vegetable oil spray. Bake in the preheated oven for 10 to 15 minutes, or until golden, turning once.

Serve hot or cold with Salads, Pickles, Chutneys and Raita of your choice (page 61).

Author's Note: Deep-fried foods are recommended for occasional eating only, even though they are made of healthful ingredients.

Nutrient Analysis (per fried Samosa):

Calories	73
Protein	5.4 gm
Carbohydrates	7.3 gm
Total Fat	2.4 gm
Saturated Fat	0.2 gm
Cholesterol	11.0 mg
Sodium with salt included	57.9 mg
Sodium with salt omitted	13.0 mg

Nutrient Analysis (per baked Samosa):

Calories	61
Protein	5.4 gm
Carbohydrates	7.3 gm
Total Fat	1.1 gm
Saturated Fat	0.1 gm
Cholesterol	11.0 mg
Sodium with salt included	57.9 mg
Sodium with salt omitted	13.0 mg

Chicken Tikka

For 4 servings you will need:

1   *cup nonfat yogurt*
2   *teaspoons garlic, minced*
2   *teaspoons ginger, minced*
1/4   *teaspoon salt (optional)*
1/2   *teaspoon ground cumin*
1/4   *teaspoon red chili powder*
1/2   *teaspoon garam masala*
1/8   *teaspoon orange food color*
1   *pinch saffron*
1   *tablespoon lemon juice*
2   *teaspoons canola oil*
1   *pound chicken breast meat, cut into 8 pieces,*
      (approx 4 ounces per serving)
1   *medium onion, peeled, sliced and separated into rings, for garnish*
1/2   *cup cilantro, chopped, for garnish*
4   *lemon wedges, for garnish*

To prepare:

1. In a bowl, combine all except the garnish ingredients and marinate for 4 to 5 hours or overnight in a refrigerator.
2. Transfer the marinade into a saucepan, cover and cook over medium heat for 15 minutes, stirring occasionally.
3. Uncover, raise heat to high and cook for further 10 minutes or until most (but not all) of the liquid has evaporated and chicken pieces are tender and juicy.

Serve on a platter, garnished with onion rings, cilantro and lemon wedges, accompanied by Naan (pages 174, 176).

Nutrient Analysis (per serving):

Calories	199
Protein	30.2 gm
Carbohydrates	9.2 gm
Total Fat	4.1 gm
Saturated Fat	0.6 gm
Cholesterol	66.8 mg
Sodium with salt included	253.6 mg
Sodium with salt omitted	119.2 mg

Marinated and Barbecued Beef Cubes
Beef Boti Kabab

For 4 servings you will need:

2   *teaspoons garlic, minced*
2   *teaspoons root ginger, minced*
1   *green chili, seeded and minced*
1/4   *cup cilantro, minced*
1/4   *teaspoon salt (optional)*
1/4   *teaspoon red chili powder (optional)*
1/2   *teaspoon garam masala*
2   *tablespoons lemon juice*
1   *pound very lean sirloin beef with all visible fat removed and cut into
     1-inch cubes (approx. 4 ounces per serving)*

To prepare:

1. In a large bowl, combine all the ingredients and marinate for 4
    to 5 hours, or overnight in a refrigerator.
2. Thread the beef cubes onto 4 skewers and broil or barbecue
    for 5 to 10 minutes, or until cooked, turning as required.

Serve with Naan (pages 174, 176) and/or Saffron Rice (page 166)
accompanied by Mixed Vegetables in Sweet and Sour Sauce (page
82), Salads, Pickles, Chutneys and Raita of your choice (page 61).

Author's Note: This dish is also known as Beef Muskaki.

Nutrient Analysis (per serving):

Calories	166
Protein	24.5 gm
Carbohydrates	2.8 gm
Total Fat	5.8 gm
Saturated Fat	2.3 gm
Cholesterol	69.2 mg
Sodium with salt included	200.9 mg
Sodium with salt omitted	67.3 mg

Exotic Beef Triangles
Beef Samosa

To make 24 you will need:

1   *pound very lean sirloin, all visible fat removed and ground*
4   *teaspoons garlic, minced*
4   *teaspoons root ginger, minced*
1/2 *teaspoon salt (optional)*
1   *green chili, seeded and finely chopped*
2   *tablespoons lemon juice*
2   *teaspoons ground coriander*
2   *teaspoons ground cumin*
1   *teaspoon garam masala*
1/4 *teaspoon red chili powder (optional)*
1½   *cups onions, finely diced*
1/2 *cup cilantro, finely chopped*
1   *recipe Samosa Pastry (see page 230)*
     canola oil for frying or vegetable oil spray for baking

To prepare filling:

1.   In a saucepan, cook beef, garlic, ginger, salt, green chili and
     lemon juice on medium heat, stirring and breaking up lumps,
     until all the liquid has evaporated. Pour the beef into a
     colander and press hard to squeeze out fat. Wrap beef in
     double paper towels and press to soak up the remaining fat.
2.   Put the drained beef in a clean saucepan and add coriander,
     cumin and garam masala. Mix well and cook for 5 to 7
     minutes, stirring frequently, until spices are blended in.
     Remove from heat.
3.   When cool, add onions and cilantro. Mix well and set aside.

Exotic Beef Triangles
Beef Samosa

To make Samosa:

1. Follow instructions for folding and filling Samosa on page 232. Then follow either Step 2 **or** Step 3 below.
2. In a deep frying pan, heat oil and deep fry triangles (Samosa) slowly, turning frequently, until golden. Remove with a slotted spoon and drain in a colander lined with paper towels.

- OR -

3. Preheat oven to 400° F. Place Samosa on a baking tray and spray lightly with vegetable oil spray. Turn over the Samosa and again spray lightly with vegetable oil spray. Bake in the preheated oven for 10 to 15 minutes, or until golden, turning once.

Serve hot or cold with Salads, Pickles, Chutneys and Raita of your choice (page 61).

Author's Note: Deep-fried foods are recommended for occasional eating only, even though they are made of healthful ingredients.

Nutrient Analysis (per fried Samosa):

Calories	76
Protein	5.0 gm
Carbohydrates	7.0 gm
Total Fat	3.0 gm
Saturated Fat	0.5 gm
Cholesterol	11.5 mg
Sodium with salt included	56.5 mg
Sodium with salt omitted	11.7 mg

Nutrient Analysis (per baked Samosa):

Calories	64
Protein	5.0 gm
Carbohydrates	7.0 gm
Total Fat	1.7 gm
Saturated Fat	0.4 gm
Cholesterol	11.5 mg
Sodium with salt included	56.5 mg
Sodium with salt omitted	11.7 mg

Marinated and Barbecued Lamb Cubes
Lamb Boti Kabab

For 4 servings you will need:

2   *teaspoons garlic, minced*
2   *teaspoons root ginger, minced*
1   *green chili, seeded and minced*
1/4   *cup cilantro, minced*
1/4   *teaspoon salt (optional)*
1/4   *teaspoon red chili powder (optional)*
1/2   *teaspoon garam masala*
2   *tablespoons lemon juice*
1   *pound boned lean leg of lamb with all visible fat removed and cut into 1-inch cubes (approx. 4 ounces per serving)*

To prepare:

1.   In a large bowl, combine all the ingredients and marinate for 4 to 5 hours or overnight in a refrigerator.
2.   Thread the lamb cubes onto 4 skewers, and broil or barbecue for 10 to 12 minutes or until cooked, turning as required.

Serve with Naan (pages 174, 176) and/or Saffron Rice (page 166) accompanied by Mixed Vegetables in Sweet and Sour Sauce (page 82), Salads, Pickles, Chutneys and Raita of your choice (page 61).

Author's Note: This dish is also known as Lamb Muskaki.

Nutrient Analysis (per serving):

Calories	164
Protein	23.7 gm
Carbohydrates	2.8 gm
Total Fat	5.9 gm
Saturated Fat	2.1 gm
Cholesterol	74.8 mg
Sodium with salt included	207.8 mg
Sodium with salt omitted	73.4 mg

Fish Kabab

For 4 servings you will need:

2   *teaspoons garlic, minced*
1   *green chili, seeded and minced*
1/4 *cup cilantro, minced*
1/4 *teaspoon salt (optional)*
2   *teaspoons canola oil*
2   *tablespoons lemon juice*
1   *pound halibut steaks, cut into 1-inch cubes*
    (approx. 4 ounces per serving)
3/4 *green pepper, cut into square pieces*
    freshly ground black pepper to taste

To prepare:

1. In a bowl, combine and mix garlic, green chili, cilantro, salt, oil and lemon juice.
2. Add fish cubes, mix well, cover and marinate in the refrigerator for 30 minutes.
3. Sprinkle marinate with black pepper and mix.
4. On 4 skewers, thread fish cubes and green pepper alternately, starting and finishing with green pepper, and broil for 3 minutes. Turn the skewers and broil for further 3 minutes or until the fish is cooked but not dry.

Serve on a bed of Pea Pilav (page 100) accompanied by Salad with Lemon Dressing (page 63).

Nutrient Analysis (per serving):

Calories	159
Protein	24.1 gm
Carbohydrates	3.4 gm
Total Fat	5.0 gm
Saturated Fat	0.5 gm
Cholesterol	36.3 mg
Sodium with salt included	196.3 mg
Sodium with salt omitted	61.9 mg

Salads, Pickles, Chutneys and Raita

Onion and Tomato Salad
Kachumber

For 4 Servings you will need:

1   *cup onions, cut into thin round slices*
1/8 *teaspoon salt (optional)*
1   *cup tomatoes, diced*
1   *green chili, seeded and chopped finely*
1/8 *teaspoon red chili powder (optional)*
1/4 *cup cilantro, finely chopped*
1/2 *teaspoon cumin seeds*
2   *tablespoons lemon or lime juice **or** vinegar*

To prepare:

1. In a bowl, separate onion rings. Sprinkle with salt and mix.
2. Add tomatoes, green chili, red chili powder, cilantro, and lemon juice or vinegar. Mix well.
3. Rub cumin seeds between palms of your hands to release flavor and sprinkle over the Kachumber.
4. Toss and serve.

Serve with any curry or rice dish.

Nutrient Analysis (per serving):

Calories	30
Protein	1.1 gm
Carbohydrates	6.9 gm
Total Fat	0.4 gm
Saturated Fat	0 gm
Cholesterol	0 mg
Sodium with salt included	73.5 mg
Sodium with salt omitted	6.1 mg

Salad with Lemon Dressing

For 6 servings you will need:

1   *cup onions peeled, cut into thin round slices*
1/4 *teaspoon salt (optional)*
2   *cups tomatoes, diced*
1/2 *cup cucumber, cut into thin rounds*
1   *cup carrots, peeled and cut into thin rounds*
1   *cup radishes, thinly sliced*
1/2 *green bell pepper, thinly sliced*
2   *green chilies, seeded and finely chopped (optional)*
1/2 *cup cilantro, finely chopped*
1/2 *teaspoon cumin seeds*
1/2 *cup lemon (or lime) juice*
3   *cups lettuce, washed and cut into bite size pieces*
     ground black pepper to taste

To prepare:

1. In a bowl, separate onion rings. Sprinkle with salt and mix.
2. Add tomatoes, cucumber, carrots, radishes, green pepper, green chilies, and cilantro. Mix gently.
3. Rub cumin seeds between palms of your hands to release flavor and add to the mixture in the bowl.
4. Add lemon (or lime) juice, mix well and chill.
5. Just before serving add lettuce, sprinkle with black pepper and toss.

This is a delicious salad with a delightful bouquet and piquant taste. Serve with any savory dish.

Nutrient Analysis (per serving):

Calories	26
Protein	1.1 gm
Carbohydrates	6.1 gm
Total Fat	0.2 gm
Saturated Fat	0 gm
Cholesterol	0 mg
Sodium with salt included	99.4 mg
Sodium with salt omitted	9.8 mg

Spicy Vegetable Relish
Vegetable Sambhar

For 4 servings you will need:

1/2	*tablespoon canola oil*
1/2	*teaspoon black mustard seeds*
1/2	*teaspoon cumin seeds*
4	*curry leaves, broken*
2	*green chilies, slit lengthwise*
1/2	*green pepper, halved and sliced*
2	*cups cabbage, shredded*
1/2	*cup carrots, cut into 2-inch long thin strips*
1	*cup cooking apples, peeled and sliced*
1/4	*teaspoon salt (optional)*
1/4	*teaspoon ground turmeric*
1/2	*teaspoon red chili powder (optional)*
1	*teaspoon sugar (optional)*
1	*tablespoon lemon juice*

To prepare:

1. In a saucepan, heat oil and fry mustard seeds, cumin seeds and curry leaves until the seeds begin to splutter; about 15 seconds. Add green chilies, green pepper and turmeric. Cook for 1 minute, stirring constantly.
2. Add cabbage, carrots, salt, chili powder, and sugar. Mix well and cook for 5 minutes, stirring frequently.
3. Add apples, mix, cover and cook over medium heat for 5 minutes, or until the vegetables are almost cooked and almost all the water has evaporated. Remove from heat. Add lemon juice and mix well.

Serve as an accompaniment with savory dishes.

Nutrient Analysis (per serving):

Calories	63
Protein	1.2 gm
Carbohydrates	11.1 gm
Total Fat	2.3 gm
Saturated Fat	0.2 gm
Cholesterol	0 mg
Sodium with salt included	149.7 mg
Sodium with salt omitted	15.3 mg

Corn Salad

For 4 servings you will need:

1	*teaspoon canola oil*
1/2	*teaspoon black mustard seeds*
4	*curry leaves, broken*
1	*green chili, seeded and chopped*
1	*12-ounce can salt-free sweet corn, drained*
1/8	*teaspoon salt (optional)*
1/4	*teaspoon ground turmeric*
1/4	*teaspoon red chili powder (optional)*
2	*tablespoons tomato paste, salt free*
1	*tablespoon lemon juice*
1/4	*cup cilantro, finely chopped*

To prepare:

1. In a saucepan, heat oil and fry mustard seeds, curry leaves and green chilies until mustard seeds begin to splutter; about 15 seconds.
2. Carefully add corn, salt, turmeric, red chili powder, and tomato paste. Mix well and cook for 2 minutes.
3. Lower the heat, cover and simmer for 5 minutes.
4. Add lemon juice and mix. Garnish with cilantro and serve.

Serve hot or cold as an accompaniment to snacks and starters. Corn Salad also makes a perfect accompaniment to cold cuts and salads. It can also be served with Chapati (page 170).

Nutrient Analysis (per serving):

Calories	116
Protein	3.5 gm
Carbohydrates	24.2 gm
Total Fat	2.6 gm
Saturated Fat	0.3 gm
Cholesterol	0 mg
Sodium with salt included	87.7 mg
Sodium with salt omitted	20.6 mg

Spicy Sprouted Mung Salad

For 6 servings you will need:

1   *recipe Sprouted Mung (see page 229)*
1   *teaspoon canola oil*
1/2 *teaspoon whole black mustard seeds*
1   *small dry red chili*
3   *curry leaves, broken*
1   *pinch asafetida (optional)*
1/2 *teaspoon salt (optional)*
1   *teaspoon sugar*
1/4 *teaspoon ground turmeric*
2   *teaspoons garlic, minced*
2   *teaspoons root ginger, minced*
1   *green chili, seeded and finely chopped*
2   *tablespoons lemon juice*
1/2 *teaspoon cumin seeds, coarsely ground*

To prepare:

1. Rinse Sprouted Mung in cold water and drain.
2. In a saucepan, heat canola oil and fry mustard seeds, dry red chili and curry leaves until the seeds begin to splutter.
3. Add asafetida and Sprouted Mung and mix gently.
4. Add 1 cup of water, salt, sugar, turmeric, garlic, ginger, and green chili and stir. Bring to boil. Reduce heat slightly, cover and cook for 15 to 20 minutes, stirring occasionally.
5. Add lemon juice and cumin seeds, mix and serve.

Serve hot or cold as a side dish, or with Breads of your choice (page 169).

As a variation mix with 1 cup nonfat yogurt and serve.

Nutrient Analysis (per serving):

Calories	30
Protein	1.5 gm
Carbohydrates	4.9 gm
Total Fat	1.0 gm
Saturated Fat	0.1 gm
Cholesterol	0 mg
Sodium with salt included	181.1 mg
Sodium with salt omitted	2.0 mg

Black-eyed Peas Salad

For 6 servings you will need:

1   *cup black-eyed peas, sorted, washed and soaked overnight*
5   *cups water*

Ingredients for the dressing:
1   *teaspoon garlic, minced*
1   *small onion, finely chopped*
1/2 *teaspoon salt (optional)*
1/2 *teaspoon sugar*
1/4 *teaspoon red chili powder (optional)*
     freshly ground black pepper to taste
2   *tablespoons lemon juice*
2   *tablespoons vinegar*

1/2 *teaspoon cumin seeds*
1/4 *cup cilantro, finely chopped*

To prepare:

1. Drain and rinse black-eyed peas. In a large saucepan, bring peas and water to boil and cook for 10 minutes, skimming off any froth that forms. Reduce heat slightly, cover and cook for 30 minutes or until the peas are soft.
2. In a bowl, mix dressing ingredients.
3. Drain and rinse the cooked peas under hot water, transfer to a glass bowl and immediately pour the dressing on the peas.
4. Rub cumin seeds between the palms of your hands, sprinkle over the salad and fold in. Cover and leave to marinate for 2 hours, stirring once or twice. Refrigerate until ready to serve.
5. Garnish with cilantro before serving.

Nutrient Analysis (per serving):

Calories	127
Protein	8.4 gm
Carbohydrates	22.9 gm
Total Fat	0.8 gm
Saturated Fat	0.2 gm
Cholesterol	0 mg
Sodium with salt included	198.5 mg
Sodium with salt omitted	19.3 mg

Carrot Pickle

For 6 servings you will need:

1   *tablespoon black mustard seeds, coarsely crushed*
1/2 *teaspoon salt (optional)*
1   *teaspoon sugar*
1/4 *teaspoon ground turmeric*
1/4 *teaspoon red chili powder (optional)*
1   *large clove garlic, minced*
1   *cup tarragon or white vinegar*
2   *cups carrots, peeled and cut into 2-inch long strips*
4   *green chilies, seeded and cut into long strips*
1/2 *green pepper, halved and cut into strips*

To prepare:

1. In a bowl, combine mustard seeds, salt, sugar, turmeric, red chili powder, garlic and vinegar, and beat well.
2. Add carrots, chilies, and green pepper. Mix thoroughly and allow the pickle to stand for 1 hour.
3. Refrigerate until ready to serve.

Carrot Pickle is a most delicious universal pickle that can be served with almost any savory dish.

Nutrient Analysis (per serving):

Calories	43
Protein	1.3 gm
Carbohydrates	9.7 gm
Total Fat	0.7 gm
Saturated Fat	0.1 gm
Cholesterol	0 mg
Sodium with salt included	192.2 mg
Sodium with salt omitted	13.1 mg

Mint Chutney
Fudina Chutney

For 1/2 cup (8 1-tablespoon servings) you will need:

1   *cup tightly packed mint leaves, washed*
1-2 *green chilies, seeded*
1/4 *teaspoon salt (optional)*
1/2 *teaspoon sugar*
4   *tablespoons lemon juice (or to taste)*

To prepare:

1.   Blend all the ingredients to a smooth paste.
2.   Pour into a glass bowl, cover and chill until ready to serve.

Serve with Snacks and Starters, or any curry dish. Also try Mint Chutney sandwiches.

Variations:

1.   Use equal amounts (1/2 cup each) of mint and cilantro.
2.   Add 1/2 cup peeled, cored and blended cooking apples.
3.   Add 1/2 cup peeled, cored and blended unripe mangos.

Nutrient Analysis (per serving):

Calories	6
Protein	0.2 gm
Carbohydrates	1.5 gm
Total Fat	0 gm
Saturated Fat	0 gm
Cholesterol	0 mg
Sodium with salt included	68.2 mg
Sodium with salt omitted	1.6 mg

Cilantro Chutney
Dhania Chutney

For 1/2 cup (8 1-tablespoon servings) you will need:

1   *cup tightly packed cilantro, washed*
1-2 *green chilies, seeded*
1/4 *teaspoon salt (optional)*
4   *tablespoons lemon juice (or to taste)*

To prepare:

1. Blend all the ingredients to a smooth paste.
2. Pour into a glass bowl and chill until ready to serve.

Serve with Snacks and Starters, or any curry dish. Also try Cilantro Chutney sandwiches.

Variations:
1. Add 1 tablespoon of minced root ginger.
2. Substitute 1/2 cup of Tamarind Sauce for lemon juice.
3. Add 1/2 cup peeled, cored, blended cooking apples.
4. Add 1/2 cup peeled, seeded, blended unripe mangos.

Nutrient Analysis (per serving):

Calories	5
Protein	0.2 gm
Carbohydrates	1.3 gm
Total Fat	0 gm
Saturated Fat	0 gm
Cholesterol	0 mg
Sodium with salt included	68.2 mg
Sodium with salt omitted	1.0 mg

Tamarind Chutney

For 16 servings you will need:

4   cups Tamarind Sauce (see page 227)
1/2 cup cilantro, crushed to a smooth paste with
1   seeded green chili
1/2 teaspoon red chili powder (optional)
1   teaspoon cumin seeds, freshly ground
1/4 teaspoon salt (optional)
2   teaspoons sugar or 1 walnut size piece of jaggery
1   carrot, finely grated

To prepare:

1.   Combine all ingredients together.   Mix well, and chill until
      ready to serve.

Tamarind Chutney makes an exciting sweet and sour dip for
savory hors d'oeuvres and snacks. It also makes a delicious salad
dressing.

Nutrient Analysis (per serving):

Calories	22
Protein	0.3 gm
Carbohydrates	5.7 gm
Total Fat	0.1 gm
Saturated Fat	0 gm
Cholesterol	0 mg
Sodium with salt included	38.0 mg
Sodium with salt omitted	5.1 mg

Date Chutney

For 16 servings you will need:

1   *recipe Tamarind Sauce (see page 227)*
1   *cup dates, pitted and finely chopped*
1/4 *teaspoon salt (optional)*
1/2 *teaspoon red chili powder (optional)*
1   *teaspoon cumin seeds, freshly ground*

To prepare:

1. In a saucepan, combine Tamarind Sauce, dates, salt and chili powder. Bring to boil and cook for 10 minutes, stirring occasionally. Remove from heat.
2. Add cumin and mix well. When cool, chill until ready to use.

Date Chutney makes an exciting sweet and sour dip for savory hors d'oeuvres and snacks.

Nutrient Analysis (per serving):

Calories	48
Protein	0.5 gm
Carbohydrates	12.7 gm
Total Fat	0.1 gm
Saturated Fat	0 gm
Cholesterol	0 mg
Sodium with salt included	36.7 mg
Sodium with salt omitted	3.9 mg

Yogurt Chutney

For 4 servings you will need:

1/2 *cup cilantro*
1-2 *green chilies (seeded)*
1/8 *teaspoon salt*
1   *teaspoon sugar (optional)*
1   *cup nonfat yogurt*
1/2 *teaspoon cumin seeds, freshly ground*
     freshly ground black pepper to taste

To prepare:

1. Blend cilantro, green chilies, salt and sugar into a smooth paste.
2. Add yogurt and mix to a smooth consistency.
3. Chill until ready to serve.
4. Garnish with cumin and black pepper just before serving.

Serve with any savory dish, or use as a salad dressing

Nutrient Analysis (per serving):

Calories	41
Protein	3.6 gm
Carbohydrates	6.6 gm
Total Fat	0.2 gm
Saturated Fat	0.1 gm
Cholesterol	1.0 mg
Sodium with salt included	111.8 mg
Sodium with salt omitted	44.6 mg

Apple Chutney

For 8 servings you will need:

4   *cooking apples*
2   *tablespoons lemon juice*
2   *teaspoons canola oil*
2   *1-inch sticks cinnamon*
2   *whole cloves*
1/2 *teaspoon black mustard seeds*
1   *small whole dry red chili*
4   *curry leaves, broken*
1/4 *teaspoon ground turmeric*
1/8 *teaspoon salt (optional)*
1/4 *cup sugar*
1/4 *teaspoon chili powder (optional)*

To prepare:

1. Peel, core and shred apples. In a bowl, mix apples and lemon juice. Set aside.
2. In a saucepan, heat oil and fry cinnamon, cloves, mustard seeds, dry red chili and curry leaves until mustard seeds begin to splutter; about 30 seconds.
3. Add turmeric immediately followed by apples with lemon juice, salt, sugar, and chili powder. Mix well and cook for 5 to 7 minutes, stirring occasionally, until almost all the liquid is absorbed.
4. Remove from heat, pour into a glass bowl. Discard the whole red chili. Refrigerate when cool.

Serve with curry dishes, cold meat and fish salads and sandwiches. Please discard whole spices when eating.

Nutrient Analysis (per serving):

Calories	70
Protein	0.3 gm
Carbohydrates	15.2 gm
Total Fat	1.4 gm
Saturated Fat	0.1 gm
Cholesterol	0 mg
Sodium with salt included	34.7 mg
Sodium with salt omitted	1.2 mg

Carrot Chutney

For 8 servings you will need:

2   *cups carrots, peeled and chopped*
1   *cup tart cooking apples, peeled, cored and chopped*
2   *green chilies, seeded*
2   *cloves garlic*
1/2 *green pepper, chopped*
1/2 *cup cilantro*
1/4 *cup lemon juice*
1/4 *teaspoon salt (optional)*
4   *tablespoons tomato paste without salt*

To prepare:

1. In a blender, process all the ingredients except tomato paste to a near smooth mixture.
2. Fold in tomato paste, mix well, and chill until ready to serve.

Serve with savory dishes, cold cuts, meats, fish, salads and sandwiches.

Nutrient Analysis (per serving):

Calories	34
Protein	0.9 gm
Carbohydrates	8.3 gm
Total Fat	0.2 gm
Saturated Fat	0 gm
Cholesterol	0 mg
Sodium with salt included	82.6 mg
Sodium with salt omitted	14.9 mg

Cucumber Raita

For 8 servings you will need:

2   *cups nonfat yogurt*
1/4 *cup cilantro*
1   *green chili, seeded*
2   *cloves garlic*
     freshly ground black pepper to taste
2   *cups cucumber, grated or finely chopped*
1   *teaspoon cumin seeds, freshly ground*
1/2 *teaspoon paprika*

To prepare:

1. In a bowl, beat yogurt to a smooth consistency.
2. In a blender, process cilantro, green chili and garlic to a smooth paste. Add to the yogurt.
3. Fold in black pepper and cucumber.
4. Cover and chill until ready to serve.
5. Before serving, garnish with coarsely ground cumin seeds and paprika.

Serve with any savory dish.

Nutrient Analysis (per serving):

Calories	40
Protein	3.6 gm
Carbohydrates	6.1 gm
Total Fat	0.2 gm
Saturated Fat	0.1 gm
Cholesterol	1.0 mg
Sodium	45.1 mg

Eggplant Raita

For 8 servings you will need:

1   *pound eggplant, washed and dried*
1   *teaspoon canola oil*
2   *teaspoons garlic, minced*
2   *green chilies, seeded and chopped*
1   *cup spring onions, chopped*
1   *teaspoon cumin seeds, coarsely ground*
1/2 *cup cilantro, chopped*
1/2 *cup tomatoes, finely chopped*
1/2 *teaspoon salt (optional)*
   freshly ground black pepper to taste
2   *cups nonfat yogurt*

To prepare:

1. Preheat oven to 350° F.
2. Brush eggplant lightly with oil, prick 2 or 3 times with a fork and bake in the preheated oven for 40 to 45 minutes.
3. Drain liquid, if any, and mash eggplant with a fork.
4. In a bowl, combine mashed eggplant with all the remaining ingredients except yogurt. Mix well.
5. Beat the yogurt, pour it over the eggplant and fold in.

Serve with Chapati (page 170) or toasted sour dough as an appetizer, or as an accompaniment with any curry dish.

Nutrient Analysis (per serving):

Calories	60
Protein	4.4 gm
Carbohydrates	10.2 gm
Total Fat	0.6 gm
Saturated Fat	0.1 gm
Cholesterol	1.0 mg
Sodium with salt included	183.1 mg
Sodium with salt omitted	48.7 mg

Spinach Raita

For 8 servings you will need:

1   *pound spinach, washed and trimmed*
2   *cups nonfat yogurt*
    freshly ground black pepper to taste
1   *teaspoon freshly ground cumin seeds*
1/4 *teaspoon salt (optional)*

To prepare:

1. In a large saucepan, bring water to boil and blanch spinach for 2 minutes or until the spinach leaves wilt.
2. Remove and drain in a colander. Press and squeeze to remove excess water.
3. Chop roughly or blend to a coarse mixture.
4. In a glass bowl, beat yogurt until smooth.
5. Add spinach and the remaining ingredients, fold in, cover and refrigerate until ready to serve.

Serve as a salad or a side dish.

Nutrient Analysis (per serving):

Calories	45
Protein	4.9 gm
Carbohydrates	6.5 gm
Total Fat	0.4 gm
Saturated Fat	0.1 gm
Cholesterol	1.0 mg
Sodium with salt included	155.3 mg
Sodium with salt omitted	88.1 mg

Main Dishes
Vegetarian

Vegetables:

Mixed Vegetable Curry	80
Mixed Vegetables in Sweet and Sour Sauce*	82
Dry Mixed Vegetable Curry*	84
Cauliflower Curry*	86
Zucchini and Eggplant Curry*	88
Curried Spinach	89
Peas and Nonfat Cheese Curry *(Matar Paneer)*	90
Spinach and Nonfat Cheese Curry *(Palakh Paneer)*	92
Corn Curry*	94
Curried Okra *(Bhindi Saag)**	95
Bitter Melon Curry *(Karela Nu Saag)*	96
Eggplant Raita Curry	98
Curried Eggplant Paté *(Bhartha)*	99
Peas Pilav	100
Vegetable Biryani	102

Daals (Lentils):

Plain Daal	104
Lentils with Mustard Seeds *(Daal with Mustard Seeds)*	106
Spinach with Split Chickpeas *(Palakh Chana Daal)*	108
Lentils with Vegetables *(Sambar)*	110
Spiced Yogurt *(Kadhi)*	112

Peas and Beans:

Mung Bean Curry	114
Chickpeas in Dry Curry Sauce *(Chana Vagharia)**	116
Chickpeas in Spicy Sauce *(Chana Masala)*	118
Black-eyed Peas Curry *(Chora nu Saag)*	120
Whole Black Mung in Spiced Yogurt *(Khata Urad)*	122

Dishes marked with * can be served as side dishes
or as salad accompaniments.

Mixed Vegetable Curry

For 8 servings you will need:

Ingredients for the spice mixture:
1/2 *cup onions, finely diced*
4   *teaspoons garlic, minced*
2   *cups tomatoes, fresh or canned without salt, finely chopped*
4   *tablespoons tomato paste without salt*
6   *teaspoons ground coriander*
3   *teaspoons ground cumin*
1   *teaspoon garam masala*
1/4 *teaspoon ground turmeric*
3/4 *teaspoon salt (optional)*
1/4 *teaspoon red chili powder (optional)*
----

2   *tablespoons canola oil*
1   *cup onions, diced*
1   *cup green beans, cut into small pieces*
1   *pound eggplant, cut into cubes*
1   *cup peas*
1   *pound potatoes, peeled and cubed*
2½   *cups water*
1/4 *cup cilantro, chopped, for garnish*

To prepare:

1. In a bowl, assemble the spice mixture ingredients.
2. In a saucepan, heat oil and sauté onions until golden.
3. Carefully, add the spice mixture, mix well and cook for 5 minutes, stirring frequently. Add a little water if the mixture becomes too dry.

Mixed Vegetable Curry

4. Add green beans, mix, cover and cook over medium heat for 10 minutes, stirring occasionally. Add a little water if the mixture becomes too dry.
5. Add the remaining vegetables and 2½ cups water. Mix well, cover and cook for 10 to 15 minutes, or until the potatoes are done.
6. Garnish with cilantro and serve.

Serve with your choice of bread (page 169) and/or rice (page 163), accompanied by Pickles, Chutneys and Raita of your choice (page 61).

Nutrient Analysis (per serving):

Calories	133
Protein	3.8 gm
Carbohydrates	22.6 gm
Total Fat	4.3 gm
Saturated Fat	0.3 gm
Cholesterol	0 mg
Sodium with salt included	219.1 mg
Sodium with salt omitted	18.0 mg

Mixed Vegetables
In Sweet And Sour Sauce

For 8 servings you will need:

1   *pound potatoes*
1   *cup peas*
1   *cup green beans, cut into small pieces*

Ingredients for the spice mixture:
2   *cups tomatoes, fresh or canned without salt, blended*
4   *tablespoons tomato paste without salt*
1/2 *teaspoon salt (optional)*
1   *teaspoon sugar*
1/2 *teaspoon ground turmeric*
1/2 *teaspoon red chilli powder (optional)*
----
2   *tablespoons canola oil*
1   *teaspoon whole black mustard seeds*
1-2 *green chillies, seeded and cut into small pieces*
6   *curry leaves*
2   *tablespoons lemon juice*
1/4 *cup cilantro, finely chopped*

To prepare:

1. Boil unpeeled potatoes until just cooked; drain. When cool, peel, cube, and set aside.
2. Boil peas and beans until almost cooked. Drain and set aside
3. In a bowl, mix together the spice mixture ingredients.
4. In a saucepan, heat oil and fry whole mustard seeds, green chilies and curry leaves until the seeds splutter; about 15 seconds.
5. Carefully add the spice mixture from the bowl, immediately cover and cook for 1 minutes.
6. Reduce heat, stir and cook, uncovered, for 5 minutes, stirring frequently.
7. Add boiled potatoes and vegetables. Mix well, cover and cook over low heat for 5 minutes.
8. Remove from heat, add lemon juice, mix, garnish with cilantro and serve.

Mixed Vegetables
In Sweet And Sour Sauce

Serve hot with your choice of breads (page 169) and/or rice (page 163), accompanied by Salads, Pickles, Chutneys and Raita of your preference (page 61). Serve hot or cold as a side dish with cold cuts or with Fish Rolls in Green Sauce (page 133).

Nutrient Analysis (per serving):

Calories	113
Protein	2.9 gm
Carbohydrates	17.7 gm
Total Fat	4.1 gm
Saturated Fat	0.3 gm
Cholesterol	0 mg
Sodium with salt included	148.1 mg
Sodium with salt omitted	13.7 mg

Dry Mixed Vegetable Curry

For 8 servings you will need:

Ingredients for the spice mixture:
2   *teaspoons garlic, minced*
2   *teaspoons root ginger, minced*
2   *cups tomatoes, fresh or canned without salt, finely chopped*
2   *tablespoons tomato paste without salt*
2   *teaspoons ground coriander*
2   *teaspoons ground cumin*
1/4   *teaspoon ground turmeric*
1/4   *teaspoon red chili powder (optional)*
3/4   *teaspoon salt (optional)*
1   *teaspoon sugar*

----
2   *tablespoons canola oil*
1/2   *teaspoon whole black mustard seeds*
1/2   *teaspoon ajma (omum) seeds (optional)*
1   *green chili, slit*
4   *curry leaves*
1   *pound eggplant, (long variety), cut into small cubes*
1   *cup peas*
1   *cup green beans, cut into small pieces*
1   *pound potatoes, peeled and cut into small cubes*
1   *cup water*
2   *tablespoons lemon juice*
1/4   *cup cilantro, finely chopped*

To prepare:

1.   In a bowl, assemble and mix the spice mixture ingredients.
2.   In a saucepan, heat oil and fry mustard seeds, ajma seeds, green chili and curry leaves until the seeds splutter; about 15 seconds.
3.   Carefully add the spice mixture, mix well, and cook for 5 minutes, stirring frequently.

Dry Mixed Vegetable Curry

4. Add eggplant, peas, beans, potatoes and 1/2 cup water. Stir well, cover and cook over medium heat until vegetables are done; about 20 minutes. Stir occasionally. If the curry becomes too dry add a little water.
5. Remove from heat, add lemon juice and cilantro. Mix and serve.

Serve with bread of your choice (page 169) accompanied by Salads, Pickles, Chutneys and Raita of your preference (page 61). This dish also makes a wonderful vegetable side dish or a salad accompaniment.

Nutrient Analysis (per serving):

Calories	126
Protein	3.5 gm
Carbohydrates	21.0 gm
Total Fat	4.1 gm
Saturated Fat	0.3 gm
Cholesterol	0 mg
Sodium with salt included	215.0 mg
Sodium with salt omitted	13.0 mg

Cauliflower Curry

For 4 servings you will need:

Ingredients for the spice mixture:
2	*teaspoons garlic, minced*
1/2	*teaspoon salt (optional)*
2	*teaspoons ground coriander*
1	*teaspoon ground cumin*
1/4	*teaspoon ground turmeric*
1/4	*teaspoon red chili powder (optional)*
2	*cups tomatoes, fresh or canned without salt, finely chopped*
2	*tablespoons tomato paste without salt*
1	*teaspoon sugar*

1	*tablespoon canola oil*
1/2	*teaspoon whole black mustard seeds*
1/4	*teaspoon cumin seeds*
1	*green chili, seeded and cut into pieces*
4	*curry leaves, broken*
1	*pound cauliflower florets*
1/2	*pound potatoes, peeled and cut into small cubes*
1	*cup peas, fresh or frozen*
1/4	*cup water*
2	*tablespoons lemon juice*
1/4	*cup cilantro, finely chopped*

To prepare:

1. In a bowl, combine the spice mixture ingredients.
2. In a saucepan, heat oil and fry mustard seeds, cumin seeds, green chili, curry leaves until mustard seeds begin to splutter; about 15 seconds.
3. Carefully add the spice mixture and mix well. Cook for 5 minutes, stirring occasionally.

Cauliflower Curry

4. Add cauliflower, potatoes, peas and 1/4 cup water. Stir well, cover and cook over medium heat for 10 minutes or until potatoes are done. If the curry becomes too dry add a little water.
5. Remove from heat. Add lemon juice and cilantro, mix and serve.

Serve with bread of your choice (page 169) accompanied by Salads, Pickles, Chutneys and Raita of your preference (page 61). This dish also makes a wonderful vegetable side dish or a salad accompaniment.

Nutrient Analysis (per serving):

Calories	179
Protein	7.2 gm
Carbohydrates	31.1 gm
Total Fat	4.7 gm
Saturated Fat	0.4 gm
Cholesterol	0 mg
Sodium with salt included	304.7 mg
Sodium with salt omitted	36.0 mg

Zucchini and Eggplant Curry

For 6 servings you will need:

1 *tablespoon canola oil*
2 *cups onions, quartered and finely sliced*
1 *teaspoon cumin seeds*
2 *cups zucchini, sliced into rounds*
3 *cups eggplant, long variety, sliced into rounds*
1/2 *green pepper, chopped*
1/2 *red pepper, chopped*
2 *cups tomatoes, fresh or canned without salt, blended*
4 *teaspoons garlic, minced*
1/2 *teaspoon salt (optional)*
1/4 *teaspoon ground turmeric*
2 *teaspoons ground coriander*
1 *teaspoon ground cumin*
   ground black pepper to taste

To prepare:

1. In a saucepan, heat canola oil and sauté onions and cumin seeds, stirring occasionally, until onions begin to soften; about 2 minutes.
2. Add remaining ingredients and mix well.
3. Reduce heat, cover and simmer for 20 minutes or until the vegetables are cooked. Stir occasionally.

Serve with bread (page 169) and/or rice (page 163) of your choice. This dish also makes a wonderful vegetable side dish or a salad accompaniment.

Nutrient Analysis (per serving):

Calories	81
Protein	2.5 gm
Carbohydrates	13.2 gm
Total Fat	3.0 gm
Saturated Fat	0.2 gm
Cholesterol	0 mg
Sodium with salt included	189.5 mg
Sodium with salt omitted	10.3 mg

Curried Spinach

For 4 servings you will need:

Ingredients for the spice mixture:

2   *teaspoons garlic, minced*
1/4 *teaspoon ground turmeric*
4   *teaspoons ground coriander*
2   *teaspoons ground cumin*
1/4 *teaspoon red chili powder (optional)*
1   *cup tomatoes, fresh or canned without salt, finely chopped*
1   *tablespoon tomato paste, without salt*
1/4 *teaspoon salt (optional)*

----

1   *tablespoon canola oil*
1   *cup onions, finely diced*
3/4 *pound potatoes, peeled and cut into small cubes*
1   *pound spinach, chopped, fresh or frozen*
2   *cups water*

To prepare:

1. In a bowl, assemble the spice mixture ingredients.
2. In a saucepan, heat oil and fry onions until they begin to brown.
3. Add the spice mixture from the bowl, mix well, and cook for 5 minutes.
4. Add potatoes, spinach, and water. Mix well, cover and cook for 10 minutes, or until the potatoes are done.

Serve with bread (page 169) and/or rice (page 163) of your choice accompanied by Lassi (page 203).

Nutrient Analysis (per serving):

Calories	164
Protein	6.6 gm
Carbohydrates	27.8 gm
Total Fat	4.8 gm
Saturated Fat	0.4 gm
Cholesterol	0 mg
Sodium with salt included	238.6 mg
Sodium with salt omitted	104.2 mg

Peas and Nonfat Cheese Curry
Matar Paneer

For 4 servings you will need:

1   *recipe Paneer (see page 224)*
    canola oil for frying Paneer

Ingredients for the spice mixture:
1/4   *teaspoon salt (optional)*
1/8   *teaspoon ground turmeric*
2   *teaspoons ground cumin*
1/2   *teaspoon garam masala*
1/4   *teaspoon red chili powder (optional)*
1   *cup tomatoes, fresh or canned without salt, blended*
2   *tablespoons tomato paste without salt*

----

1   *tablespoon canola oil*
1   *cup onions, finely diced*
2   *teaspoons garlic, minced*
2   *teaspoons root ginger, minced*
1   *green chili, seeded and chopped*
2   *cups peas, frozen or fresh*
1½   *cups water*
1/4   *cup cilantro, finely chopped*

To prepare:

1. Cut Paneer into 1/2-inch squares. In a frying pan, heat canola oil and shallow fry Paneer, turning over as required, until light golden. Drain on paper towels and set aside.
2. In a bowl, assemble the spice mixture ingredients.
3. In a saucepan, heat 1 tablespoon oil and sauté onions, garlic, ginger and green chili, stirring frequently, until onions are soft.
4. Add the spice mixture from the bowl, mix well and cook for 5 minutes, stirring frequently. If the mixture becomes too dry, add a little water.
5. Add peas and water, mix well and bring to boil. Lower heat slightly, cover and cook for 10 minutes.

Peas and Nonfat Cheese Curry
Matar Paneer

6. Add the Paneer pieces, mix, cover and cook for 10 minutes.
7. Serve garnished with cilantro.

Serve with bread (page 169) and/or rice (page 163) of your choice, accompanied by Salads, Pickles, Chutneys and Raita of your preference (page 61).

Nutrient Analysis (per serving):

Calories	310
Protein	22.4 gm
Carbohydrates	45.5 gm
Total Fat	5.2 gm
Saturated Fat	0.9 gm
Cholesterol	8.8 mg
Sodium with salt included	402.9 mg
Sodium with salt omitted	268.5 mg

Spinach and Nonfat Cheese Curry
Palakh Paneer

For 5 servings you will need:

1	*recipe Paneer (see page 224)*
	canola oil for frying Paneer

Ingredients for the spice mixture:

2	*teaspoons ground coriander*
1	*teaspoon ground cumin*
1/4	*teaspoon ground turmeric*
1/4	*teaspoon red chili powder (optional)*
1/2	*teaspoon garam masala*
1/8	*teaspoon salt (optional)*
1	*cup tomatoes, fresh or canned without salt, blended*
1	*tablespoon tomato paste without salt*

1/2	*tablespoon oil*
2	*teaspoons garlic, minced*
2	*teaspoons root ginger, minced*
1	*small onion, finely diced*
2	*pounds spinach, chopped, fresh or frozen*
1½	*cups water*
1/4	*cup cilantro*

To prepare:

1. Cut Paneer into 1/2-inch squares. In a frying pan, heat canola oil and shallow fry Paneer, turning over as necessary, until light golden. Drain on paper towels and set aside.
2. In a bowl, combine spice mixture ingredients.
3. In a saucepan, heat 1/2 tablespoon oil and sauté garlic and ginger for 30 seconds.
4. Carefully add the spice mixture from the bowl, mix and cook for 5 minutes, stirring frequently. If the mixture becomes too dry, add a little water.
5. Add spinach and water, mix well, cover and cook over medium heat for 10 minutes.

Spinach and Nonfat Cheese Curry
Palakh Paneer

6.   Add the Paneer pieces, mix well, cover and cook over
     medium heat for 5 minutes.
7.   Garnish with cilantro and serve.

Serve with bread (page 169) and/or rice (page 163) of your choice,
accompanied by Salads, Pickles, Chutneys and Raita of your
preference (page 61).

Nutrient Analysis (per serving):

Calories	222
Protein	19.7 gm
Carbohydrates	32.8 gm
Total Fat	3.2 gm
Saturated Fat	0.7 gm
Cholesterol	7.1 mg
Sodium with salt included	405.0 mg
Sodium with salt omitted	53.8 mg

Corn Curry

For 6 servings you will need:

Ingredients for the spice mixture:

3   *teaspoons garlic, minced*
4   *teaspoons ground coriander*
2   *teaspoons ground cumin*
1/8 *teaspoon ground turmeric*
1/2 *teaspoon garam masala*
1/4 *teaspoon red chili powder (optional)*
2   *cups tomatoes, fresh or canned without salt, finely chopped*
2   *tablespoons paste, without salt*
1/2 *teaspoon salt (optional)*

----

1   *tablespoon canola oil*
1   *cup onions, finely diced*
3   *cups water*
3   *corn on the cob, cut into 6 pieces*
3/4 *pound potatoes, peeled and cut into 12 pieces*
1/4 *cup cilantro, finely chopped*

To prepare:
1. In a bowl, combine all the spice mixture ingredients.
2. In saucepan, heat oil and sauté onions until golden.
3. Carefully add the spice mixture from the bowl, mix well and cook for 5 minutes. Add a little water if mixture is too dry.
4. Add water, corn and potatoes. Cover and cook over medium heat until corn and potatoes are done; about 15 minutes.
5. Garnish with cilantro and serve.

Serve with bread and/or rice of your choice (pages 169, 163), accompanied by Salad with Lemon Dressing (page 63).

Nutrient Analysis (per serving):

Calories	138
Protein	3.9 gm
Carbohydrates	26.1 gm
Total Fat	3.4 gm
Saturated Fat	0.3 gm
Cholesterol	0 mg
Sodium with salt included	198.8 mg
Sodium with salt omitted	19.6 mg

Curried Okra
Bhindi Saag

For 6 servings you will need:

Ingredients for the spice mixture:
1/4 *teaspoon ground turmeric*
1/2 *teaspoon red chili powder (optional)*
3/4 *teaspoon garam masala*
2   *teaspoons garlic, minced*
1   *green chili*
2   *cups tomatoes, fresh or canned without salt, finely chopped*
2   *tablespoons tomato paste without salt*
1/2 *teaspoon salt (optional)*
----

1   *tablespoon canola oil*
2   *cups onions, quartered and finely sliced*
1   *pound okra, rinsed and patted dry with paper towel, topped &
     tailed, and cut into half lengthwise and then halved*
1/4 *cup cilantro, finely chopped*

To prepare:

1. In a bowl, assemble the spice mixture ingredients.
2. In a saucepan, heat oil and sauté onions until soft.
3. Add the spice mixture from the bowl, mix and cook for 5
    minutes, stirring occasionally. Add a little water if too dry.
4. Add okra, mix well, cover, and cook over medium heat for 10
    minutes. Garnish with cilantro and serve

Serve with bread of your choice (page 169) and nonfat yogurt
accompanied by Salads, Pickles and Chutneys of your preference
(page 61), or serve as a side dish.

Nutrient Analysis (per serving):

Calories	94
Protein	3.2 gm
Carbohydrates	15.7 gm
Total Fat	2.8 gm
Saturated Fat	0.2 gm
Cholesterol	0 mg
Sodium with salt included	195.3 mg
Sodium with salt omitted	16.1 mg

Bitter Melon Curry
Karela Nu Saag

For 6 servings you will need:

1	*pound karela (bitter melon)*
1/2	*teaspoon salt (for treating karela)*

Ingredients for the spice mixture:

2	*teaspoons garlic, crushed*
1/2	*teaspoon salt (optional)*
2	*cups tomatoes, fresh or canned without salt, finely chopped*
2	*tablespoons tomato paste without salt*
2	*teaspoons ground coriander*
1	*teaspoon ground cumin*
1/8	*teaspoon ground turmeric*
1/2	*teaspoon garam masala*

3	*tablespoons canola oil*
2	*cups onions, finely sliced*
1	*tablespoon lemon juice*

To prepare:

1. Peel karela with a potato peeler and cut into 1/4-inch thick round slices. Place in a bowl and rub with 1/2 teaspoon salt. Set aside for at least half an hour.
2. Wash karela thoroughly in cold water and drain.
3. Boil karela in hot water for 10 minutes and drain well.
4. In a bowl, assemble the spice mixture ingredients.
5. In a saucepan, heat oil and sauté onions until soft. Discard oil.
6. Add spice mixture, mix well and cook for 5 minutes, stirring frequently. Add a little water if the mixture becomes too dry.
7. Add karela, mix well, lower heat, cover and cook for 10 minutes, stirring occasionally. Add a little water if too dry.
8. Add lemon juice, mix and serve.

Bitter Melon Curry
Karela Nu Saag

Serve with bread of your choice (page 169) accompanied by
Salads, Pickles, Chutneys and Raita of your preference (page 61),
or serve as a side dish.

Nutrient Analysis (per serving):

Calories	87
Protein	5.6 gm
Carbohydrates	12.1 gm
Total Fat	3.4 gm
Saturated Fat	0.2 gm
Cholesterol	0 mg
Sodium with salt included	197.7 mg
Sodium with salt omitted	19.2 mg

Eggplant Raita Curry

For 6 servings you will need:

1   *tablespoon canola oil*
1   *cup onions, finely diced*
1   *teaspoon cumin seeds*
1   *pound eggplant, washed and cut into small cubes*
2   *teaspoons garlic, minced*
1/2 *teaspoon salt (optional)*
1/8 *teaspoon ground turmeric*
1   *cup tomatoes, finely chopped*
1   *cup nonfat yogurt*
    freshly ground black pepper to taste
1/4 *cup cilantro, finely chopped, for garnish*
1   *green chili, seeded and finely chopped, for garnish*

To prepare:

1. In a saucepan, heat oil and sauté onions and cumin seeds until the onions are transparent.
2. Add the remaining ingredients except yogurt and black pepper, stir well, cover and cook over medium heat for 15 minutes or until the eggplant is cooked.
3. Add yogurt, black pepper, mix well and cook for further 5 minutes.
4. Garnish with cilantro and chilies and serve.

Serve with bread of your choice (page 169), or as a side dish with any meat or vegetable curry.

Nutrient Analysis (per serving):

Calories	82
Protein	3.7 gm
Carbohydrates	12.0 gm
Total Fat	2.7 gm
Saturated Fat	0.3 gm
Cholesterol	0.7 mg
Sodium with salt included	213.9 mg
Sodium with salt omitted	34.7 mg

Curried Eggplant Paté
Bhartha

For 4 servings you will need:

1 *pound eggplant, washed and dried*

Ingredients for the spice mixture:

2 *teaspoons garlic, minced*
1 *green chili, seeded and finely chopped*
1 *cup tomatoes, finely chopped*
1/4 *teaspoon salt (optional)*
1/8 *teaspoon ground turmeric*
2 *teaspoons ground coriander*
2 *teaspoons ground cumin*
1/4 *teaspoon red chili powder (optional)*

1/2 *tablespoon canola oil*
1 *cup onions, finely diced*
1/4 *cup cilantro*

To prepare:

1. Preheat oven to 350° F.
2. Brush eggplant lightly with oil, prick with fork 2 or 3 times and bake in the preheated oven for 40 to 45 minutes.
3. When cool, chop eggplant roughly or blend. Drain liquid.
4. In a bowl, combine all the spice mixture ingredients.
5. In a saucepan, heat oil and sauté onions until soft.
6. Add the spice mixture from the bowl, mix well and cook for 5 minutes. Add chopped eggplant and cilantro, mix well, and cook for another 5 minutes.

Serve with nonfat yogurt and bread of your choice (page 169). Bhartha makes a delicious hors d'oeuvre with toasted bread.

Nutrient Analysis (per serving):

Calories	85
Protein	2.8 gm
Carbohydrates	15.5 gm
Total Fat	2.5 gm
Saturated Fat	0.2 gm
Cholesterol	0 mg
Sodium with salt included	146.6 mg
Sodium with salt omitted	12.2 mg

Peas Pilav

For 8 servings you will need:

Ingredients for the spice mixture:

1½	*cups peas, fresh or frozen*
1/4	*cup lowfat yogurt*
2	*cups tomatoes, fresh or canned without salt, finely chopped*
4	*teaspoons garlic, minced*
4	*teaspoons root ginger, minced*
1/2	*teaspoon salt (optional)*
1/4	*teaspoon ground turmeric*
2	*teaspoons ground coriander*
1	*teaspoon ground cumin*
1	*teaspoon garam masala*

2	*tablespoons canola oil*
1	*cup onions, finely diced*
1-2	*green chilies*
2	*1-inch sticks cinnamon*
16	*whole black peppercorns*
2	*teaspoons cumin seeds*
3	*cups water (approximately)*
3/4	*teaspoon salt (optional)*
3/4	*pound potatoes, cut into 16 pieces*
1/4	*cup cilantro, finely chopped*
2	*cups Basmati rice*

To prepare:

1. In a bowl, combine all the spice mixture ingredients.
2. In a large saucepan, heat oil and sauté onions, green chilies, cinnamon stick, peppercorns and cumin until the onions start turning gold.
3. Pour the spice mixture from the bowl into the saucepan, stir, cover, and cook for 10 minutes over medium heat, stirring occasionally.
4. Add water (to make 4 cups of liquid in all), salt, cilantro and potatoes. Stir well, cover, and bring to boil.

Peas Pilav

5. Wash and drain rice. Add to the saucepan, stir gently, partially cover and cook until almost all the water has been absorbed; about 10 minutes.
6. Reduce heat to low, cover and cook for 10 to 15 minutes, or until the rice is done.

Serve with Salads, Pickles, Chutneys or Raita of your choice (page 61). Peas Pilav is also ideal as a side dish, or for a cold buffet.

Please discard whole spices when eating.

Nutrient Analysis (per serving):

Calories	291
Protein	7.2 gm
Carbohydrates	55.6 gm
Total Fat	4.6 gm
Saturated Fat	0.5 gm
Cholesterol	0.4 mg
Sodium with salt included	352.4 mg
Sodium with salt omitted	14.9 mg

Vegetable Biryani

For 8 servings you will need:

For Biryani masala:

Ingredients for the spice mixture:
1   *cup tomatoes, fresh or canned without salt, blended*
1/2 *cup tomato paste without salt*
2   *teaspoons garlic, minced*
2   *teaspoons ginger, minced*
1   *cup lowfat yogurt*
1/4 *teaspoon salt (optional)*
1/8 *teaspoon saffron*
2   *green chilies*
1/2 *cup onions, finely chopped*
2   *teaspoons garam masala*

1/2 *pound potatoes, peeled and cut into 8 pieces*
2   *cups onions, finely sliced*
     canola oil for frying onions
1   *pound eggplant (long variety), cut into round slices*
1   *pound zucchini, cut into round slices*
1/2 *green pepper, chopped*
1/2 *red pepper, chopped*
1   *cup cauliflower florets*

For Saffron Rice:
2½   *cups Basmati rice*
1¼   *teaspoons salt*
5   *cups water*
1/8 *teaspoon saffron*
1/4 *teaspoon yellow food color*
2   *1-inch sticks cinnamon*
4   *whole cardamoms*
4   *whole cloves*

Vegetable Biryani

To prepare:

Biryani Masala
1. In a saucepan, combine the spice mixture ingredients and cook over low heat for 15 minutes.
2. Boil potatoes and set aside.
3. In a frying pan, heat oil and fry sliced onions until golden brown. Lift with a slotted spoon and drain on paper towel. Add drained onion to the spice mixture in the saucepan.
4. Add vegetables, mix, cover and cook over low heat for 20 minutes, or until the vegetables are done.
5. Add boiled potatoes and mix well, cover and set aside.

Saffron Rice
1. In a large saucepan, bring 4-3/4 cups water to boil.
2. Wash rice several times and drain. Add to the boiling water.
3. Add salt, cover saucepan partially and bring to boil again.
4. Cook until almost all the water is absorbed, about 5 to10 minutes.
5. Reduce heat to low, cover and cook for 10 minutes.
6. In 1/4 cup of water, mix yellow color and saffron, and pour over the rice. Fold the rice gently, cover and cook for 5 minutes or until the rice is done.
7. In a small saucepan, heat 1 tablespoon oil left from frying onions. Fry cinnamon, cardamoms and cloves for 1 minute. Pour over the rice and cover immediately. Remove from heat.

Serve Biryani Masala on a bed of saffron rice, accompanied by Salads, Pickles and Raita of your choice (page 61).

Nutrient Analysis (per serving):

Calories	371
Protein	9.5 gm
Carbohydrates	70.0 gm
Total Fat	6.6 gm
Saturated Fat	0.9 gm
Cholesterol	1.7 mg
Sodium with salt included	445.5 mg
Sodium with salt omitted	42.4 mg

Plain Daal

For 6 servings you will need:

1/2 cup mung daal (split and hulled mung lentil)
1/2 cup masoor daal (split and hulled red lentil)
1/4 cup channa daal (split and hulled chickpeas)
6   cups water

Ingredients for the spice mixture:
4   teaspoons garlic, minced
4   teaspoons root ginger, minced
1   green chili, seeded and finely chopped
2   cups tomatoes, fresh or canned without salt, finely chopped
2   teaspoons cumin seeds, freshly crushed
2   teaspoons ground coriander
1/4 teaspoon ground turmeric
1/2 teaspoon garam masala
1/4 teaspoon red chili powder (optional)
3/4 teaspoon salt (optional)

----

1   tablespoon canola oil
1   cup onions, finely diced
1   1-inch stick cinnamon
2   whole cloves
1/4 cup cilantro, chopped
2   tablespoons lemon juice

To prepare:

1. Sort and wash lentils in water several times. Drain.
2. In a large saucepan, boil lentils in water for 10 minutes, skimming off any froth that forms. Reduce heat slightly, cover and cook for 20 to 25 minutes, or until lentils are tender.
3. Blend until smooth. Set aside.
4. In a bowl, assemble the spice mixture ingredients.
5. In a large saucepan, heat oil and sauté onions, cinnamon stick and cloves, stirring frequently, until onions begin to brown.

Plain Daal

6. Carefully add the spice mixture from the bowl, stir well, and cook for 5 minutes, stirring frequently.
7. Add the blended lentils and cilantro. Stir well, and bring to boil. If the Daal is too thick, add some water.
8. Lower heat, cover the saucepan, and simmer for 10 minutes.
9. Add lemon juice, mix and serve.

Serve hot with bread (page 169) and/or rice (page 163) of your choice accompanied by Salads, Pickles, Chutneys and Raita of your preference (page 61).

Please discard whole spices when eating.

This Daal can also be served on its own as a delicious soup.

Note: 1¼ cups of any one variety of lentils can be used, if preferred, instead of the three specified in the recipe.

Nutrient Analysis (per serving):

Calories	195
Protein	12.7 gm
Carbohydrates	31.5 gm
Total Fat	3.3 gm
Saturated Fat	0.3 gm
Cholesterol	0 mg
Sodium with salt included	280.0 mg
Sodium with salt omitted	11.3 mg

Lentils with Mustard Seeds
Daal with Mustard Seeds

For 6 servings you will need:

1/2   *cup mung daal (split and hulled mung)*
1/2   *cup masoor daal (split and hulled red lentils)*
1/4   *cup channa daal (split and hulled chickpeas)*
6   *cups water*
\-
Ingredients for the spice mixture:
4   *teaspoons garlic, minced*
4   *teaspoons root ginger, minced*
3/4   *teaspoon salt (optional)*
1   *teaspoon sugar*
1/4   *teaspoon ground turmeric*
1   *teaspoon ground cumin*
1/4   *teaspoon red chili powder (optional)*
2   *cups tomatoes, fresh or canned without salt, finely chopped*
\-
1   *tablespoon canola oil*
1/2   *teaspoon whole black mustard seeds*
1   *cup onions, finely diced*
1-2   *green chilies, slit lengthwise*
6   *curry leaves, broken*
1/4   *cup cilantro, finely chopped*
2   *tablespoons lemon juice*

To prepare:

1. Sort and wash lentils in water several times. Drain.
2. In a large saucepan, boil lentils in water for 10 minutes, skimming off any froth that forms. Reduce heat slightly, cover and cook for 20 to 25 minutes, or until tender.
3. Blend until smooth. Pour back into the saucepan and set aside.
4. In a bowl, assemble the spice mixture ingredients.
5. In a small saucepan, heat oil and fry mustard seeds until they begin to splutter, about 15 seconds.

Lentils with Mustard Seeds
Daal with Mustard Seeds

6. Add onions, green chillies and curry leaves. Sauté for 1 minute, stirring frequently. Do not let the onions brown.
7. Carefully add the spice mixture from the bowl; mix well, and cook for 5 minutes, stirring occasionally.
8. Pour the cooked spice mixture into the saucepan with the blended lentils and mix well. Add cilantro, cover, and simmer for 10 minutes. Add some water if the Daal becomes too thick.
9. Add lemon juice, mix and serve.

Serve hot with bread (page 169) and/or rice (page 163) of your choice accompanied by Salads, Pickles, Chutneys and Raita of your preference (page 61).

This Daal can also be served on its own as a delicious soup.

Note: 1¼ cups of any one variety of lentil can be used, if preferred, instead of the three specified in the recipe.

Nutrient Analysis (per serving):

Calories	191
Protein	12.5 gm
Carbohydrates	30.5 gm
Total Fat	3.2 gm
Saturated Fat	0.3 gm
Cholesterol	0 mg
Sodium with salt included	278.8 mg
Sodium with salt omitted	11.5 mg

Spinach with Split Chickpeas
Palakh Chana Daal

For 6 servings you will need:

1   *cup chana daal (split, hulled chickpeas)*
4   *cups water*

Ingredients for the spice mixture:
3   *teaspoons garlic, minced*
3   *teaspoons root ginger, minced*
1/2 *teaspoon salt (optional)*
4   *teaspoons ground coriander*
3   *teaspoons ground cumin*
1/4 *teaspoon ground turmeric*
1/4 *teaspoon red chili powder (optional)*
1   *cup tomatoes, fresh or canned without salt, finely chopped*
2   *tablespoons tomato paste without salt*

----

1   *tablespoon canola oil*
1   *cup onions, finely diced*
1   *teaspoon cumin seeds*
1/2 *pound spinach, chopped, fresh or frozen*
1/2 *teaspoon garam masala*
1   *green chili, seeded and finely chopped (optional)*
1/4 *teaspoon cilantro, finely chopped*
1   *tablespoon lemon juice*

To prepare:

1. Clean and wash split chickpeas in water several times and drain.
2. In a large saucepan, boil daal in water for 10 minutes, skimming off any froth that forms. Lower heat slightly, cover and cook for 30 minutes or until daal is soft. Add a little water if necessary.
3. In a bowl, combine spice mixture ingredients.
4. In another saucepan, heat oil and sauté onions and cumin until onions begin to brown.
5. Add spice mixture from the bowl, cook for 5 minutes stirring frequently. If the mixture become too dry, add a little water.

Spinach with Split Chickpeas
Palakh Chana Daal

6. Add spinach, stir and cook for 5 minutes.
7. Add cooked chickpeas with any liquid that is left plus 1/4 cup of water. Mix well, cover and cook for 10 minutes.
8. Add lemon juice, garam masala, chopped green chilies and cilantro. Mix and serve.

Serve hot with bread (page 169) and/or rice (page 163) of your choice accompanied by Salads, Pickles, Chutneys and Raita of your preference (page 61).

Nutrient Analysis (per serving):

Calories	188
Protein	9.0 gm
Carbohydrates	29.4 gm
Total Fat	5.3 gm
Saturated Fat	0.5 gm
Cholesterol	0 mg
Sodium with salt included	226.4 mg
Sodium with salt omitted	47.2 mg

Lentils with Vegetables
Sambar

For 8 servings you will need:

1   cup toor daal *(split and hulled pigeon peas)*
6   cups water
1   tablespoon canola oil
1/2 teaspoon whole black mustard seeds
1   teaspoon cumin seeds
6   curry leaves, broken
1   cup onions, quartered and sliced
1-2 green chilies, seeded and chopped
1/4 teaspoon ground turmeric
2   teaspoons ground coriander
1   cup tomatoes, chopped
2   cups zucchini, cut into round slices
1   cup carrots, cut into round slices
1   cup green bell pepper, cut into pieces
3/4 teaspoon salt (optional)
1/4 teaspoon red chili powder
1/2 cup Tamarind Sauce (see page 227)

To prepare:

1. Clean and wash toor daal in warm water several times and drain.
2. In a large saucepan, boil daal in water for 10 minutes, skimming off any froth that forms. Reduce heat slightly, cover and cook for 20 to 25 minutes, or until lentils are soft.
3. In another saucepan, heat oil and fry mustard seeds, cumin seeds and curry leaves until the seeds begin to splutter; about 15 seconds.
4. Add onions, green chilies, turmeric and coriander, and sauté for 1 minute, stirring all the time.
5. Add tomatoes, vegetables, salt and red chili powder, and cook for 10 minutes, stirring frequently.
6. Transfer to the simmering lentils, add Tamarind Sauce, mix well, cover and cook over medium heat for 10 minutes.

Lentils with Vegetables
Sambar

Serve with Dosa (page 179), Idli (page 180) or bread of your choice (page 169).

Variation: Mung daal can be used instead of Toor daal

Nutrient Analysis (per serving):

Calories	140
Protein	6.9 gm
Carbohydrates	24.2 gm
Total Fat	2.6 gm
Saturated Fat	0.3 gm
Cholesterol	0 mg
Sodium with salt included	214.3 mg
Sodium with salt omitted	12.7 mg

Spiced Yogurt
Kadhi

For 6 servings you will need:

6   tablespoons gram (chickpea) flour
4   cups water
2   cups nonfat yogurt
1/2 teaspoon salt (optional)
1   teaspoon sugar, or a walnut size jaggery
1/4 teaspoon ground turmeric
1   teaspoon ground cumin
2   teaspoons garlic, minced
1   tablespoon canola oil
1   clove garlic, thinly sliced
1/2 teaspoon whole mustard seeds
1/2 teaspoon fenugreek seeds
2   whole cloves
4   curry leaves, broken
1/4 cup onions, finely diced
1   green chili (optional)
1/4 cup cilantro, finely chopped
1   tablespoon lemon juice

To prepare:

1. In a large bowl, sift gram flour and make a thick, smooth batter with 1/2 cup of water, added a little at a time. Add the remaining water, yogurt, salt, sugar, turmeric, cumin, and garlic. Blend or whisk thoroughly.
2. In a saucepan, heat oil and fry garlic, mustard seeds, fenugreek seeds, cloves and curry leaves until the mustard seeds begin to splutter; about 15 seconds.
3. Add the yogurt mixture and stir continuously until the mixture comes to boil.
4. Reduce heat, add onions and green chili, cover partially, and simmer for 15 minutes, stirring occasionally.
5. Add cilantro and lemon juice, stir and serve.

Spiced Yogurt
Kadhi

Serve with Chuti Khichdi (page 167), Lissi Khichdi (page 168), Chapati (page 170), or Rotlo (page 178).

Kadhi can also be served on its own as a delicious soup.

Nutrient Analysis (per serving):

Calories	144
Protein	8.4 gm
Carbohydrates	19.7 gm
Total Fat	3.9 gm
Saturated Fat	0.4 gm
Cholesterol	1.4 mg
Sodium with salt included	241.5 mg
Sodium with salt omitted	62.3 mg

Mung Bean Curry

For 4 servings you will need:

1   cup whole mung beans, sorted, washed and soaked overnight
5   cups water

Ingredients for the spice mixture:
2   teaspoons garlic, minced
1/2   teaspoon salt (optional)
2   teaspoons ground coriander
1   teaspoon ground cumin
1/8   teaspoon ground turmeric
1/2   teaspoon garam masala
1/4   teaspoon red chili powder (optional)
1   cup tomatoes, fresh or canned without salt, finely chopped
2   tablespoons tomato paste without salt
----
1   tablespoon canola oil
1   cup onions, finely diced
2   tablespoons lemon juice
1/4   cup cilantro, finely chopped

To prepare:

1.   Drain, rinse and drain mung beans.
2.   In a large saucepan, boil drained mung beans in water for 10 minutes skimming off any froth that forms.   Lower heat slightly, cover and cook for 30 minutes, or until mung beans are tender.
3.   In a bowl, assemble the spice mixture ingredients.
4.   In another saucepan, heat oil and sauté onions until soft.
5.   Add the spice mixture from the bowl and cook for 5 minutes, stirring frequently. If the mixture becomes too dry, add a little water.
6.   Add cooked mung beans along with the liquid, mix well. Bring to boil, immediately lower heat and simmer for 10 to 15 minutes. If curry becomes too dry add a little water.
7.   Add lemon juice and mix . Garnish with cilantro, and serve.

Mung Bean Curry

Serve with bread of your choice (page 169) and/or Plain Rice (page 164), and nonfat yogurt, accompanied by Salads, Pickles and Chutneys of your choice (page 61).

Nutrient Analysis (per serving):

Calories	248
Protein	13.8 gm
Carbohydrates	40.5 gm
Total Fat	4.8 gm
Saturated Fat	0.5 gm
Cholesterol	0 mg
Sodium with salt included	286.6 mg
Sodium with salt omitted	17.9 mg

Chickpeas in Dry Curry Sauce
Chana Vagharia

For 6 servings you will need:

1   *cup dark brown chickpeas, sorted, washed and soaked overnight*

Ingredients for the spice mixture:
2   *teaspoons garlic, minced*
2   *teaspoons root ginger, minced*
1/4 *teaspoon ground turmeric*
3   *teaspoons ground coriander*
3   *teaspoons ground cumin*
1/4 *teaspoon red chili powder*
1/2 *teaspoon salt (optional)*
1   *teaspoon sugar*
2   *cups tomatoes, fresh or canned without salt, blended*
3   *tablespoons tomato paste without salt*
----
1   *tablespoon canola oil*
1   *teaspoon cumin seeds*
1/2 *teaspoon black mustard seeds*
4   *curry leaves, broken*
1/2 *cup water*
1   *tablespoon lemon juice*
1   *green chili, seeded and finely chopped*
1/4 *cup cilantro, finely chopped*

To prepare:

1.   Drain, rinse and drain chickpeas.
2.   In a large saucepan, boil chickpeas in water for 50 minutes or
     until soft. Drain.
3.   In a bowl, assemble spice mixture ingredients.
4.   In another saucepan, heat oil and fry cumin seeds, mustard
     seeds and curry leaves until seeds begin to splutter; about 15
     seconds.

Chickpeas in Dry Curry Sauce
Chana Vagharia

5. Add spice mixture from the bowl. Mix and cook for 5 minutes, stirring frequently. If the mixture becomes too dry, add a little water.
6. Add chickpeas, stir well, cover and cook over medium heat for 10 minutes, stirring occasionally.
7. Add 1/2 cup water, cover and simmer for 10 to 15 minutes, stirring occasionally. If the mixture becomes too dry, add a little water.
8. Add lemon juice and stir. Garnish with green chili and cilantro, and serve.

Serve on its own, with bread of your choice (page 169) accompanied by Salads and Chutneys of your preference (page 61), as a side dish or as a salad accompaniment.

Nutrient Analysis (per serving):

Calories	181
Protein	8.0 gm
Carbohydrates	28.4 gm
Total Fat	5.2 gm
Saturated Fat	0.4 gm
Cholesterol	0 mg
Sodium with salt included	199.8 mg
Sodium with salt omitted	19.7 mg

Chickpeas in Spicy Sauce
Chana Masala

For 4 servings you will need:

1   *15½-ounce can low-salt garbanzo (chickpeas)*
1   *tablespoon canola oil*
1   *teaspoon cumin seeds*
1   *cup onions, finely diced*
2   *teaspoons ground coriander*
1/8 *teaspoon ground turmeric*
1   *teaspoon garam masala*
1/2 *teaspoon salt (optional)*
2   *teaspoons garlic, minced*
2   *teaspoons ginger, minced*
1   *cup water*
3   *tablespoons tomato paste without salt*
1   *tablespoon lemon juice*
1/4 *teaspoon red chili powder (optional)*

For Garnish:

1   *green chili, seeded and chopped*
1/2 *cup onions, sliced*
1   *cup tomatoes, sliced*
1/4 *cup cilantro, chopped*

To prepare:

1. Rinse garbanzo beans in cold water and drain.
2. In a saucepan, heat oil and fry cumin seeds for a few seconds. Add onions and fry until they begin to brown.
3. Lower heat. Add coriander, turmeric, garam masala, salt, garlic and ginger. Mix and cook for 30 seconds, stirring all the time.
4. Add 1 cup water and tomato paste. Mix and bring to boil.
5. Add garbanzo beans, lemon juice and red chili powder. Mix well, cover and cook over medium heat for 15 minutes, or until garbanzo beans are soft, stirring occasionally. If the mixture gets too dry, add a little water.
6. Serve garnished with green chilies, onions, tomatoes and cilantro.

Chickpeas in Spicy Sauce
Chana Masala

Serve with bread of your choice (page 169) accompanied by Salad with Lemon Dressing (page 61).

Nutrient Analysis (per serving):

Calories	275
Protein	12.3 gm
Carbohydrates	44.3 gm
Total Fat	7.1 gm
Saturated Fat	0.6 gm
Cholesterol	0 mg
Sodium with salt included	291.3 mg
Sodium with salt omitted	22.6 mg

Black-eyed Peas Curry
Chora nu Saag

For 6 servings you will need:

1¼ cups black-eyed peas, sorted, washed and soaked overnight
6   cups water

Ingredients for the spice mixture:
2   teaspoons garlic, minced
1/2 teaspoon salt (optional)
2   teaspoons ground coriander
1   teaspoon ground cumin
1/4 teaspoon ground turmeric
1/2 teaspoon garam masala
1/2 teaspoon red chili powder (optional)
1   cup tomatoes, fresh or canned without salt, finely chopped
2   tablespoons tomato paste without salt

----

1   tablespoon canola oil
1   cup onions, finely diced
1½   cups water
2   tablespoons lemon juice
1/4 cup cilantro, finely chopped

To prepare:

1. Drain, rinse and drain black-eyed peas.
2. In a large saucepan, boil the peas in water for 10 minutes, skimming off any froth that forms. Reduce heat slightly, cover and cook for further 20 minutes, or until the peas are soft. Drain.
3. Combine the spice mixture ingredients in a bowl.
4. In a separate saucepan, heat oil and sauté onions until they just begin to brown.
5. Add the spice mixture from the bowl, stir well and cook for 5 minutes, stirring occasionally. If the mixture becomes too dry, add a little water.
6. Add the drained black-eyed peas and 1½ cups water. Bring to boil, lower the heat, cover and cook for 15 minutes.
7. Add lemon juice, mix, garnish with cilantro and serve.

Black-eyed Peas Curry
Chora nu Saag

Serve with bread (page 169) and/or rice (page 163) of your choice, accompanied by Salads, Pickles, Chutneys and Raita of your preference (page 61). Serve also as a side dish or salad accompaniment.

Nutrient Analysis (per serving):

Calories	192
Protein	11.0 gm
Carbohydrates	31.2 gm
Total Fat	3.6 gm
Saturated Fat	0.4 gm
Cholesterol	0 mg
Sodium with salt included	210.3 mg
Sodium with salt omitted	31.1 mg

Whole Black Mung In Spiced Yogurt
Khata Urad

For 8 servings you will need:

1   *cup whole urad lentils, sorted, washed and soaked overnight*
6   *cups water*

Ingredients for the yogurt mixture:
3   *tablespoons chickpea flour (besan)*
2   *cups water*
2   *cups nonfat yogurt*
1/4 *teaspoon ground turmeric*
1/4 *teaspoon red chili powder (optional)*
1   *teaspoon coarsely ground cumin seeds*
3/4 *teaspoon salt*
2   *teaspoons sugar*

----

1   *teaspoon canola oil*
1/2 *teaspoon whole black mustard seeds*
1/2 *teaspoon cumin seeds*
1   *pinch asafetida (optional)*
2   *green chilies*
2   *tablespoons lemon juice*
1/4 *cup cilantro, finely chopped*

To prepare:

1. Drain, rinse and drain urad.
2. In a large saucepan, boil urad in water for 10 minutes, skimming of any froth that forms. Reduce heat slightly, cover and cook for further 30 minutes, or until urad is soft. Drain.
3. In a large bowl, combine the yogurt mixture ingredients. (In order to avoid lumps, first mix the chickpea flour with a little water into a smooth paste before adding the remaining ingredients).
4. In a large saucepan, heat oil and fry mustard seeds, cumin seeds and asafetida until the mustard seed splutter; about 15 seconds.

Whole Black Mung In Spiced Yogurt
Khata Urad

5. Carefully add the yogurt mixture, green chilies and drained urad, and bring to boil, stirring occasionally. Lower the heat, cover and simmer for 10 to 15 minutes.
6. Add lemon juice and cilantro. Stir and serve.

Serve with bread (page 169) and/or rice (page 163) of your choice, accompanied by Salads, Pickles, Chutneys and Raita of your preference (page 61).

Nutrient Analysis (per serving):

Calories	134
Protein	10.5 gm
Carbohydrates	21.4 gm
Total Fat	1.2 gm
Saturated Fat	0.2 gm
Cholesterol	1.0 mg
Sodium with salt included	262.8 mg
Sodium with salt omitted	61.2 mg

Main Dishes
Non-Vegetarian

Fish:

Poultry:

Meat:

Spiced Fish
Masala Macchi

For 4 servings you will need:

1   *pound steaks or fillets halibut, cut into 4 pieces,*
    (approx 4 ounces per serving)
2   *tablespoons lemon juice*
    vegetable oil spray

Ingredients for the spice mixture:
2   *cups tomatoes, fresh or canned without salt, finely chopped*
4   *tablespoons tomato paste without salt*
4   *teaspoons garlic, minced*
1/4 *teaspoon salt (optional)*
1/8 *teaspoon ground turmeric*
4   *teaspoons ground coriander*
2   *teaspoons ground cumin*
1   *teaspoon garam masala*
1/4 *teaspoon red chili powder (optional)*
1/2 *cup onions, finely diced*

----

1   *tablespoon canola oil*
3/4 *pound potatoes, peeled and cut into 16 round slices*
2   *long mild green chilies, slit lengthwise*
1/4 *cup cilantro finely chopped*

To prepare:

1. Preheat broiler.
2. Wash fish steaks and soak in lemon juice for 15 minutes.
3. Lightly spray the fish with oil on both sides and place on a broiler pan and broil for 4 minutes on each side. Set aside.
4. Boil potatoes, drain and set side.
5. In a bowl, assemble the spice mixture ingredients.
6 In a wide frying pan, heat oil. Carefully add spice mixture, mix well and cook for 5 minutes, stirring frequently. If the mixture gets too dry, add a little water.
7. Add long green chilies, lower the heat, cover and cook for 5 minutes.

Spiced Fish
Masala Macchi

8. Add boiled potatoes, cilantro and mix well. Carefully place
    the cooked fish in the center of the frying pan, pushing
    potatoes and chilies to the side. Spoon some sauce over the
    fish, cover and cook for 5 minutes, or until the dish is heated
    through.

Serve with Chapatis (page 170) or Rotlo (page 178) and lemon
wedges, or as an accompaniment with Daal (pages 104, 106) and
Rice (pages 164, 165) or Kadhi (page 112) and Chuti Khichdi (page
167), accompanied by Salad with Lemon Dressing (page 63).

Author's Tip: Other fish such as salmon, trout or white fish can
be used instead of halibut.

Nutrient Analysis (per serving):

Calories	314
Protein	27.7 gm
Carbohydrates	27.5 gm
Total Fat	11.1 gm
Saturated Fat	1.0 gm
Cholesterol	36.3 mg
Sodium with salt included	219.9 mg
Sodium with salt omitted	86.1 mg

Royal Fish Curry
Baked Fish Kalio

For 4 servings you will need:

1½ *pound whole trout, trimmed and washed,*
        (approx. 4 ounces flesh per serving)
2   *tablespoons lemon juice*

Ingredients for the spice mixture:
1   *cup tomatoes, fresh or canned without salt, blended*
1   *tablespoon tomato paste without salt*
1/2 *cup lowfat yogurt*
2   *teaspoons garlic, minced*
2   *teaspoons root ginger, minced*
1/4 *teaspoon ground turmeric*
1/4 *teaspoon red chili powder (optional)*
1/2 *teaspoon garam masala*
1/4 *teaspoon salt*

----

     canola oil for frying onions
1   *cup onions, finely diced*
1/2 *pound potatoes, peeled, washed, cut into 8 pieces and parboiled*

To prepare:

1.   Preheat oven to 400° F.
2.   Make three shallow diagonal cuts in the fish on both sides.
     Rub inside and outside with lemon juice and place in a baking
     dish.
3.   In a bowl, assemble the spice mixture ingredients.
4.   In a small saucepan, heat oil and fry onions until golden.
     Remove onions with a slotted spoon and drain on a paper
     towel. Add drained onions to the spice mixture in the bowl.
     Mix well.

Royal Fish Curry
Baked Fish Kalio

5. Spread 2 tablespoons spice mixture inside the fish and pour the rest over the fish. Cover and allow to marinate for 20 minutes.
6. Bake in the preheated oven for 15 minutes.
7. Uncover, arrange parboiled potatoes around the fish, cover and bake for further 10 minutes, or until the potatoes are done.

Serve with Chapati (page 170), Naan (pages 174, 176) and/or rice of your choice (page 163), accompanied by Salad with Lemon Dressing (page 63).

Nutrient Analysis (per serving):

Calories	254
Protein	27.2 gm
Carbohydrates	20.7 gm
Total Fat	7.0 gm
Saturated Fat	1.3 gm
Cholesterol	66.4 mg
Sodium with salt included	329.3 mg
Sodium with salt omitted	60.6 mg

Fish Curry

For 4 servings you will need:

```
-------------------------------------------
```
Ingredients for the spice mixture:
2   teaspoons garlic, minced
1/4 teaspoon salt (optional)
6   teaspoons ground coriander
4   teaspoons ground cumin
1/4 teaspoon ground turmeric
1   teaspoon garam masala
2   cups tomatoes, fresh or canned without salt, finely chopped
3   tablespoons tomato paste without salt
1/2 cup onions, finely chopped
```
-------------------------------------------
```
1   tablespoon canola oil
3   whole cloves
2   cups water
3/4 pound potatoes, peeled and cut into 12 pieces
1   pound halibut,* cleaned and cut into pieces,
     (approx 4 ounces per serving)
1   tablespoon lemon juice
1/4 cup cilantro, finely chopped

To prepare:

1.   In a bowl, assemble all the spice mixture ingredients.
2.   In a saucepan, heat oil and fry cloves for 1/2 minute.
3.   Carefully add the spice mixture from the bowl, mix well, and
     cook for 5 minutes, stirring occasionally. If the mixture
     becomes too dry, add a little water.
4.   Add water, potatoes, stir well and bring to boil. Cover and
     cook for 5 minutes.
5.   Add fish pieces, cover and bring to boil again. Reduce heat
     and simmer for 10 minutes or until the fish is cooked.
6.   Add lemon juice, stir, garnish with cilantro and serve.

Serve with Plain Rice (page 164), Chapatis (page 170), or Rotlo
(page 178), accompanied by Salad with Lemon Dressing (page 63).

Fish Curry

Please discard cloves when eating.

* Other fish such as haddock, cod, trout, red snapper, or salmon may be substituted.

Nutrient Analysis (per serving):

Calories	277
Protein	27.5 gm
Carbohydrates	26.6 gm
Total Fat	7.4 gm
Saturated Fat	0.7 gm
Cholesterol	36.3 mg
Sodium with salt included	225.1 mg
Sodium with salt omitted	93.0 mg

Delicately Spiced Fish Curry

For 4 servings you will need:

1	*pound halibut steak, cut into 4 pieces, approx. 4 ounces per serving*
2	*tablespoons lemon juice*
1	*tablespoon canola oil*
1	*cup onions, quartered and finely sliced*
4	*teaspoons garlic, crushed*
1	*cup tomatoes, fresh or canned without salt, blended*
3	*tablespoons tomato paste without salt*
1/4	*teaspoon salt (optional)*
1/4	*teaspoon ground black pepper*
1/4	*teaspoon ground turmeric*
2	*cups water*
1	*pound potatoes, peeled and cut into thick round slices*
2	*tablespoons lemon juice*
1/4	*cup cilantro, finely chopped*

To prepare:

1. Marinate fish in lemon juice for 30 minutes.
2. In a wide saucepan, heat oil and sauté onions until soft.
3. Add garlic, tomatoes, tomato paste, salt, pepper and turmeric. Mix and cook for 5 minutes, stirring frequently.
4. Add water, potatoes and mix. Place fish on top, cover and bring to boil. Reduce heat and simmer for 15 minutes, or until potatoes are done.
5. Add lemon juice, mix, garnish with cilantro and serve.

Serve with Chapati (page 170) and/or Plain Rice (page 164), accompanied by Salad with Lemon Dressing (page 63).

Nutrient Analysis (per serving):

Calories	287
Protein	27.5 gm
Carbohydrates	29.8 gm
Total Fat	6.6 gm
Saturated Fat	0.7 gm
Cholesterol	36.3 mg
Sodium with salt included	215.4 mg
Sodium with salt omitted	81.0 mg

Fish Rolls in Green Sauce

For 4 servings you will need:

4	*cloves garlic*
1-2	*green chilies, seeded*
1/2	*cup cilantro, tightly packed*
1/4	*teaspoon salt (optional)*
4	*tablespoons lemon juice*
	freshly ground black pepper to taste
1	*teaspoon canola oil*
1	*pound cod, 4 thin fillets (approx 4 ounces per serving)*

To prepare:

1. In a blender, process all the ingredients except fish into a smooth paste to make the Green Sauce.
2. Spread the Sauce on the fish fillets. Roll the fillets like Swiss rolls, with the sauce on the inside. Use wooden toothpicks to hold the fish rolls in shape.
3. Arrange the fish rolls in a coverable microwave-proof dish. Cover and cook in a microwave oven at full power for 2 minutes. Uncover, and turn over the fish rolls . Cover and cook for further 2 minutes, or until the fish flakes easily when tested with a fork.

Serve with Mixed Vegetables in Sweet and Sour Sauce (page 82), Peas Pilav (page 100), or with cooked macaroni and sauce from the Vegetable Pizza recipe (page 212), accompanied by Salad with Lemon Dressing (page 63).

Nutrient Analysis (per serving):

Calories	118
Protein	21.1 gm
Carbohydrates	3.4 gm
Total Fat	2.0 gm
Saturated Fat	0.2 gm
Cholesterol	49.7 mg
Sodium with salt included	197.6 mg
Sodium with salt omitted	63.2 mg

Shrimp Curry

For 4 servings you will need:

2	teaspoons garlic, minced
2	teaspoons root ginger, minced
1/4	teaspoon salt (optional)
2	cups tomatoes, fresh or canned without salt, finely chopped
4	tablespoons tomato paste without salt
1½	tablespoons canola oil
1	cup onions, finely diced
4	teaspoons ground coriander
2	teaspoons ground cumin
1/4	teaspoon ground turmeric
1	teaspoon garam masala
1/4	teaspoon red chili powder (optional)
1	pound cooked bay shrimps, approx 4 ounces per serving
1/2	cup green pepper, chopped
1/2	cup red pepper, chopped
1/4	cup cilantro, finely chopped
1	tablespoon lemon juice

To prepare:

1. In a bowl, mix garlic, ginger, salt, tomatoes and tomato paste, and set aside.
2. In a saucepan, heat oil and sauté onions until soft.
3. Add coriander, cumin, turmeric, garam masala, chili powder, mix and cook for 30 seconds.
4. Add the mixture from the bowl, stir well and cook for 5 minutes, stirring frequently.
5. Add shrimps, mix well, cover, reduce heat slightly and cook for 10 minutes.
6. Add green and red pepper, mix well, cover and cook for 3 minutes.
7. Add lemon juice, mix, garnish with cilantro and serve.

Serve with bread of your choice (page 169), or as an accompaniment to Daal (pages 104, 106) and Rice (pages 164, 165).

Shrimp Curry

Nutrient Analysis (per serving):

Calories	235
Protein	25.6 gm
Carbohydrates	16.2 gm
Total Fat	8.2 gm
Saturated Fat	0.9 gm
Cholesterol	172.4 mg
Sodium with salt included	324.3 mg
Sodium with salt omitted	189.9 mg

Fish Pilav

For 4 servings you will need:

Ingredients for the spice mixture:
4   *teaspoons garlic, minced*
4   *teaspoons ginger, minced*
1/2 *cup nonfat yogurt*
2   *green chilies, seeded and finely chopped*
1½   *cups tomatoes, fresh or canned without salt, finely chopped*
1/4 *cup cilantro, finely chopped*
2   *tablespoons lemon juice*
1/4 *teaspoon ground turmeric*
1/4 *teaspoon salt (optional)*

----

2   *tablespoons canola oil*
1   *cup onions, quartered and finely sliced*
12   *whole black peppercorns*
2   *teaspoons cumin seeds*
1   *pound halibut,* cleaned and cut into pieces,*
     (approx 4 ounces per serving)
3   *cups water*
1/2 *teaspoon salt (optional)*
1/2 *pound potatoes, cut into 8 pieces*
1/4 *cup cilantro, finely chopped*
1½   *cups Basmati rice*

To prepare:

1. In a bowl, assemble the spice mixture ingredients.
2. In a saucepan, heat oil and sauté onions, black peppercorns and cumin seeds until onions are soft.
3. Add the spice mixture from the bowl, mix well, and cook for 5 minutes, stirring frequently. If the mixture becomes too dry, add a little water.
4. Add fish, lower heat slightly, cover, and cook for 10 minutes or until the fish is firm. Remove saucepan from heat.
5. Gently lift out the fish, place on a plate, cover, and set aside.
6. Return the saucepan to the cooker, add water, salt, potatoes, and cilantro. Cover and bring to boil.

Fish Pilav

7. Add washed and drained rice, cover and cook for 5 minutes. Reduce heat to low and cook for further 10 minutes or until almost all the water is absorbed.
8. Place fish pieces on top of the rice, cover and cook over very low heat for further 10 minutes, or until the rice is done.

Serve with Salads, Pickles and Raita or your choice (page 61).

*Other white fish or salmon may be substituted for halibut.

Variation: Use dill weed instead of cilantro.

Nutrient Analysis (per serving):

Calories	552
Protein	33.3 gm
Carbohydrates	79.2 gm
Total Fat	10.8 gm
Saturated Fat	1.1 gm
Cholesterol	36.8 mg
Sodium with salt included	501.5 mg
Sodium with salt omitted	96.3 mg

Festive Fish and Rice
Fish Biryani

For 6 servings you will need:

For Fish masala:
1½   *pounds halibut* steaks, cut into pieces,*
     approx. 4 ounces per serving
3   *tablespoons lemon juice*
1   *teaspoon canola oil*

Ingredients for the spice mixture:
3   *teaspoons garlic, minced*
3   *teaspoons ginger, minced*
1   *teaspoon garam masala*
1/2 *teaspoon red chili powder (optional)*
1/8 *teaspoon ground turmeric*
2   *whole green chilies*
2   *cups tomatoes, fresh or canned without salt, blended*
3   *tablespoons tomato paste without salt*
1/4 *teaspoon salt (optional)*
----

     canola oil for frying onions
2   *cups onions, quartered and finely sliced*
2   *1-inch sticks cinnamon*
2   *whole cloves*
2   *whole cardamoms*
3/4 *pound potatoes, boiled, peeled & cut into 12 pieces*

For Rice:
4   *cups water*
2   *cups Basmati rice*
3/4 *teaspoon salt (optional)*

To prepare:

Fish Masala:
1.   Preheat broiler.
2.   Wash fish and marinate in lemon juice for 15 minutes.
3.   Coat fish with one teaspoon oil, place in a broiling pan and broil for 4 minutes on each side. Set aside.

Festive Fish and Rice
Fish Biryani

4. In a bowl, assemble the spice mixture ingredients.
5. In a frying pan, heat oil and fry onions until golden brown. Lift onions with a slotted spoon and drain on paper towel.
6. In a wide saucepan, heat 2 teaspoons of oil left from frying onions and fry cinnamon, cloves and cardamoms for 1 minute.
7. Carefully add the spice mixture from the bowl and cook for 5 minutes, stirring frequently. Add fried onions, mix well, reduce heat slightly, cover and cook for 3 minutes.
8. Arrange fish and boiled potatoes on the masala, spoon some masala over the fish and potatoes, cover and cook for 5 minutes or until heated through.

Rice:
1. In a large saucepan, bring water to boil.
2. Wash rice, drain and add to the boiling water.
3. Add salt, cover saucepan partially and bring to boil again. Cook until almost all the water is absorbed, about 5 to 10 minutes.
4. Reduce heat to low, cover saucepan and cook for further 10 minutes or until the rice is done.

Serve fish and masala on a bed of rice, garnished with lemon wedges, and accompanied by Salads, Pickles and Raita of your choice (page 61).

* Other fish such as haddock, cod, trout, red snapper, or salmon may be substituted.

Nutrient Analysis (per serving):

Calories	527
Protein	31.0 gm
Carbohydrates	70.9 gm
Total Fat	12.9 gm
Saturated Fat	1.2 gm
Cholesterol	36.3 mg
Sodium with salt included	443.0 mg
Sodium with salt omitted	84.7 mg

Turkey Kabab Curry

For 5 servings you will need:

Ingredients for the spice mixture:
2   teaspoons garlic, minced
2   teaspoons root ginger, minced
2   cups tomatoes, fresh or canned without salt, finely chopped
4   tablespoons tomato paste without salt
1/4 teaspoon ground turmeric
4   teaspoons ground coriander
2   teaspoons ground cumin
1   teaspoon garam masala
1/2 teaspoon salt (optional)
1/4 teaspoon red chili powder (optional)

----

2   tablespoons canola oil
1/2 cup onions, finely sliced
1   pound potatoes, peeled and cut into 15 pieces
    stock from the Boiled Turkey Kababs recipe (see page 44)
20 Kababs from the Boiled Turkey Kababs recipe (see page 44)
1/4 cup cilantro finely chopped

To prepare:

1. In a bowl, assemble the spice mixture ingredients.
2. In a large saucepan, heat oil and fry onions until golden brown.
3. Gently add the spice mixture from the bowl, mix well and cook for 5 minutes, stirring occasionally.
4. Add potatoes and stock, stir, and bring to boil. Lower heat, cover, and cook for 10 minutes, or until the potatoes are almost cooked.
5. Add turkey kababs, cover, and cook for 10 minutes.
6. Garnish with cilantro and serve.

Serve with bread (page 169) and/or rice (page 163) of your choice, accompanied by Salads, Pickles, Chutneys and Raita of your preference (page 61).

Turkey Kabab Curry

Nutrient Analysis (per serving):

Calories	285
Protein	26.6 gm
Carbohydrates	30.3 gm
Total Fat	7.2 gm
Saturated Fat	0.7 gm
Cholesterol	56.3 mg
Sodium with salt included	283.8 mg
Sodium with salt omitted	69.4 mg

Ground Turkey Pie
Mayai Mani

For 6 servings you will need:

Ingredients for the spice mixture:
2   cups tomatoes, fresh or canned without salt, finely chopped
4   tablespoons tomato paste without salt
4   teaspoons garlic, minced
4   teaspoons root ginger, minced
3/4 teaspoon salt (optional)
1   green chili, seeded and finely chopped
4   teaspoons ground coriander
2   teaspoons ground cumin
1/4 teaspoon ground turmeric
1   teaspoon garam masala
1/2 teaspoon red chili powder (optional)
----
2   tablespoons canola oil
1½   cups onions, quartered and finely sliced
1   pound ground turkey breast, approx 2-2/3 ounces per serving
1/2 pound potatoes, peeled and cut into thin round slices
1/4 cup cilantro, chopped
1/4 cup water
2   tablespoons lemon juice
5   eggs whites, beaten with a dash of freshly ground black pepper

To prepare:

1. Preheat oven to 400° F.
2. In a bowl, assemble the spice mixture ingredients.
3. In a large saucepan, heat oil and sauté onions until they begin to brown.
4. Add spice mixture from the bowl and cook for 5 minutes, stirring occasionally. If the mixture becomes too dry, add a little water.
5. Add ground turkey, mix well, and cook for 7 minutes or until the turkey is just cooked, stirring occasionally.
6. Add potatoes, cilantro, and 1/4 cup water. Mix well, cover saucepan and cook for 5 to 7 minutes.

Ground Turkey Pie
Mayai Mani

7. Add lemon juice, mix well, cover, and remove from heat.
8. In an oven-proof dish, pour half of the egg whites to cover the base. Spread the cooked turkey evenly over the egg whites. Pour the remaining egg whites evenly over the turkey.
9. Bake in the preheated oven for 10 to 15 minutes until the egg is cooked and firm.

Serve with bread of your choice (page 169), accompanied by Salads, Pickles, Chutneys and Raita of your preference (page 61).

Nutrient Analysis (per serving):

Calories	221
Protein	24.3 gm
Carbohydrates	18.6 gm
Total Fat	5.8 gm
Saturated Fat	0.6 gm
Cholesterol	46.9 mg
Sodium with salt included	366.9 mg
Sodium with salt omitted	97.6 mg

Ground Turkey and Peas Curry
Kheema Matar Curry

For 6 servings you will need:

Ingredients for the spice mixture:
3   teaspoons garlic, minced
3   teaspoons ginger, minced
1/2 teaspoon salt (optional)
1/4 teaspoon ground turmeric
3   teaspoons ground cumin
6   teaspoons ground coriander
1   teaspoon garam masala
1/2 teaspoon red chili powder (optional)
2   cups tomatoes, fresh or canned without salt, finely chopped
2   tablespoons tomato paste without salt

----

2   tablespoons canola oil
1   cup onions, finely diced
1   pound ground breast of turkey, approx. 2-2/3 ounces per serving
1½ cups water
2   cups peas
3/4 pound potatoes, peeled and diced into 18 pieces
2   tablespoons lemon juice
1/4 cup cilantro, finely chopped

To prepare:

1. In a bowl, assemble all the spice mixture ingredients.
2. In a saucepan, heat oil and fry onions until golden.
3. Carefully add the spice mixture from the bowl, mix well and cook for 5 minutes, stirring occasionally. If the mixture becomes too dry, add a little water.
4. Add ground turkey, mix well and cook for 7 minutes or until the turkey is just cooked, stirring occasionally.
5. Add 1½ cups water, peas and potatoes. Mix, cover and bring to boil. Reduce heat and cook for 10 minutes, or until potatoes are done.
6. Add lemon juice and cilantro, mix well, and serve.

Ground Turkey and Peas Curry
Kheema Matar Curry

Serve with bread (page 169) and/or rice (page 163) of your choice, accompanied by Salads, Pickles, Chutneys and Raita of your preference (page 61).

Nutrient Analysis (per serving):

Calories	246
Protein	23.8 gm
Carbohydrates	25.4 gm
Total Fat	6.0 gm
Saturated Fat	0.6 gm
Cholesterol	46.9 mg
Sodium with salt included	232.1 mg
Sodium with salt omitted	54.1 mg

Exotic Barbecued Chicken
Tandoori Chicken

For 4 servings you will need:

2	*teaspoons garlic, minced*
2	*teaspoons root ginger, minced*
1	*green chilli, seeded and minced (optional)*
1/4	*teaspoon salt (optional)*
1/2	*teaspoon ground coriander*
1	*teaspoon ground cumin*
1/4	*teaspoon red chili powder (optional)*
1	*teaspoon garam masala*
1/2	*cup lowfat yogurt*
2	*tablespoons tomato paste without salt*
1	*teaspoon canola oil*
2	*tablespoons lemon juice*
4	*5-ounce chicken breasts, skinned and all visible fat removed*

To prepare:

1. In a large bowl, combine all the ingredients except chicken and make a smooth marinade.
2. Make two diagonal cuts in each chicken breast and marinate for 3 to 4 hours or overnight in a refrigerator.
3. Broil or barbecue chicken, occasionally basting with the marinade, for 5 to 7 minutes on each side or until cooked but not dry.

Serve with Naan (pages 174, 176), Saffron Rice (page 166), Mixed Vegetables in Sweet and Sour Sauce (page 82) and Salads, Pickles, Chutneys and Raita of your choice (page 61).

Nutrient Analysis (per serving):

Calories	181
Protein	28.8 gm
Carbohydrates	8.5 gm
Total Fat	3.4 gm
Saturated Fat	0.8 gm
Cholesterol	67.5 mg
Sodium with salt included	239.8 mg
Sodium with salt omitted	105.4 mg

Dry Chicken Curry - *Karahi Chicken*

For 4 servings you will need:

Ingredients for the spice mixture:

1   *cup canned tomatoes without salt, blended*
4   *tablespoons tomato paste without salt*
3   *teaspoons garlic, minced*
3   *teaspoons root ginger, minced*
1   *small green chili, seeded and minced*
1/2   *teaspoon salt (optional)*
1/4   *teaspoon ground turmeric*
1/4   *teaspoon red chili powder*
2   *teaspoons ground cumin*
4   *teaspoons ground coriander*
1/2   *teaspoon garam masala*

----

1   *tablespoon canola oil*
1   *teaspoon fenugreek seeds*
1¼   *pound chicken breasts, skinned and cut into 12 pieces,*
      approx. 5 ounces per serving
1   *green pepper, cut into 8 pieces*

To prepare:

1. In a bowl, assemble the spice mixture ingredients.
2. In a large saucepan, heat oil and fry fenugreek seeds until they darken and begin to splutter; about 20 to 30 seconds.
3. Carefully add the spice mixture, mix and cook for 5 minutes, stirring frequently. Add chicken pieces, mix, reduce heat slightly, cover and cook for 5 minutes.
4. Add 1/2 cup water and green pepper, mix, cover and cook over medium to low heat for 20 minutes, stirring occasionally.

Serve with Chapati (page 170) or Naan (pages 174, 176).

Nutrient Analysis (per serving):

Calories	216
Protein	28.7 gm
Carbohydrates	12.8 gm
Total Fat	6.1 gm
Saturated Fat	0.7 gm
Cholesterol	65.8 mg
Sodium with salt included	362.8 mg
Sodium with salt omitted	94.1 mg

Royal Chicken Curry
Chicken Kalio

For 4 servings you will need:

Ingredients for the marinade:

1/2	*cup low fat yogurt*
1	*pinch saffron*
1	*small onion, chopped*
2	*teaspoons garlic, minced*
2	*teaspoons root ginger, minced*
1	*green chili (optional)*
1/4	*teaspoon salt (optional)*
2	*1-inch sticks cinnamon*
3	*whole cardamoms*
2	*whole cloves*
1¼	*pound chicken breasts, skinned, all visible fat removed and cut into 12 pieces, approx. 5 ounces per serving*

---

	canola oil for frying onions
2	*cups onions, quartered and finely sliced*
2	*cups tomatoes, fresh or canned without salt, blended*
3	*tablespoons tomato paste without salt*
1/2	*teaspoon ground cumin*
1/4	*teaspoon red chili powder (optional)*
1	*teaspoon garam masala*
3/4	*pound potatoes, peeled and cut into 12 pieces*
1	*cup hot water*

To prepare:

1. In a bowl, combine all the marinade ingredients and marinate chicken for at least 1 hour.
2. In a large saucepan, heat canola oil and fry onions until golden. Remove onions with a slotted spoon and drain on paper towel.
3. Discard oil from the saucepan. In the same saucepan add the marinade and tomatoes. Return saucepan to heat, cover and bring to boil. Cook for 10 minutes.

Royal Chicken Curry
Chicken Kalio

4. Add cumin, red chili powder, garam masala, fried onions and tomato paste, and stir. Reduce heat to low, cover and simmer for 10 minutes.
5. Parboil potatoes, drain and add to the simmering Kalio. Add 1 cup of hot water, stir, cover and simmer for further 5 minutes or until potatoes are cooked.

Serve with bread of your choice (page 169) and/or Saffron Rice (page 166).

Please discard whole spices when eating.

Nutrient Analysis (per serving):

Calories	377
Protein	32.1 gm
Carbohydrates	33.8 gm
Total Fat	13.1 gm
Saturated Fat	1.5 gm
Cholesterol	67.5 mg
Sodium with salt included	252.8 mg
Sodium with salt omitted	118.4 mg

Chicken Curry

For 4 servings you will need:

```
-------------------------------------------
```

Ingredients for the spice mixture:

3   *teaspoons garlic, minced*
3   *teaspoons root ginger, minced*
2   *cups tomatoes, fresh or canned without salt, finely chopped*
4   *tablespoons tomato paste without salt*
1/8 *teaspoon ground turmeric*
4   *teaspoons ground coriander*
2   *teaspoons ground cumin*
1   *teaspoon garam masala*
1/4 *teaspoon red chili powder (optional)*
1/2 *teaspoon salt (optional)*

```
-------------------------------------------
```

2   *tablespoons canola oil*
1/2 *cup onions, quartered and finely sliced*
1¼ *pounds chicken breasts, skinned, all visible*
      fat removed and cut into 8 pieces, approx 5 ounces per serving
3   *cups water*
3/4 *pounds potatoes, peeled & cut into 12 pieces*
1   *tablespoon lemon juice*
1/4 *cup cilantro, chopped*

To prepare:

1. In a bowl, assemble all the spice mixture ingredients.
2. In a large saucepan, heat oil and sauté onions until golden brown.
3. Add spice mixture from the bowl, mix well and cook for 5 minutes, stirring occasionally.
4. Add chicken pieces, mix well. Lower heat slightly, cover and cook for 15 minutes, stirring occasionally. Add a little water if the mixture gets too dry.
5. Add 3 cups water and potatoes, mix, cover, and bring to boil. Lower heat and simmer for 15 to 20 minutes, or until potatoes are cooked.

Chicken Curry

6.   Add lemon juice, cilantro, stir and serve.

Serve with bread (page 169)and/or rice (page 163) of your choice, accompanied by Salads, Pickles, Chutneys and Raita of your preference (page 61).

Nutrient Analysis (per serving):

Calories	304
Protein	29.9 gm
Carbohydrates	26.3 gm
Total Fat	9.3 gm
Saturated Fat	1.0 gm
Cholesterol	65.8 mg
Sodium with salt included	364.7 mg
Sodium with salt omitted	96.7 mg

Chicken and Lentils
Chicken Daal

For 8 servings you will need:

1/2 cup mung daal (split and hulled mung)
1/2 cup masoor daal (split and hulled red lentils)
1/4 cup channa daal (split and hulled chickpeas)
6   cups water
2   tablespoons canola oil
1   cup onions, finely diced
2   1-inch sticks cinnamon
2   whole cloves
1¼   pounds breasts of chicken, skinned, and cut into 12 pieces,
     approx. 2½ ounces per serving
4   teaspoons garlic, minced
4   teaspoons root ginger, minced
1   green chili, seeded and finely chopped
2   cups tomatoes, fresh or canned without salt, blended
3/4 teaspoon salt (optional)
4   teaspoons ground coriander
3   teaspoons ground cumin
1/4 teaspoon ground turmeric
1   teaspoon garam masala
1/4 teaspoon red chili powder (optional)
2   tablespoons lemon juice
1/4 cup cilantro, chopped

To prepare:

1. Wash lentils in water several times and drain.
2. In a large saucepan, boil lentils in water for 10 minutes, skimming off any froth that forms. Reduce heat slightly, cover and cook for 20 to 25 minutes or until the lentils are tender.
3. Blend until smooth, and set aside.
4. In a large saucepan, heat oil and sauté onions, cinnamon, and cloves until onions begin to brown.
5. Add chicken pieces, garlic, root ginger, green chili, tomatoes, and salt. Stir, cover and cook for 10 minutes.

Chicken and Lentils
Chicken Daal

6. Add coriander, cumin, turmeric, garam masala, and red chili powder. Stir well and cook for 3 minutes. Stir occasionally.
7. Carefully add the lentils, stir well, and let the mixture come to boil. Reduce heat, cover and simmer for 15 minutes. If Daal is too thick, add a little water.
8. Add lemon juice, garnish with cilantro and serve.

Serve with bread of your choice (page 169) and/or Plain Rice (page 164) or Lightly Flavored Rice (page 165), accompanied by Salads, Pickles, Chutneys and Raita of your choice (page 61).

Author's Tip: 1¼ cups of any one lentil can be used, if preferred, instead of the three.

Nutrient Analysis (per serving):

Calories	309
Protein	29.1 gm
Carbohydrates	34.9 gm
Total Fat	6.6 gm
Saturated Fat	0.8 gm
Cholesterol	43.9 mg
Sodium with salt included	330.7 mg
Sodium with salt omitted	61.9 mg

Chicken Pilav
Chicken Akni

For 8 servings you will need:

2	pounds skinless and boneless chicken breast meat, with all visible fat removed, and cut into pieces, approx 4 ounces per serving
5	teaspoons garlic, minced
5	teaspoons root ginger, minced
1-2	green chilies, seeded and finely chopped
2	cups tomatoes, finely chopped
1	teaspoon cumin seeds, coarsely crushed
1¼	teaspoons salt (optional)
2	tablespoons lemon juice
1	cup low fat yogurt
4	tablespoons canola oil
2	cups onions, quartered and finely sliced
1	whole green chili
3	1-inch sticks cinnamon
24	whole black peppercorns
2	teaspoons cumin seeds
2	whole cardamoms
1	pound potatoes, peeled and cut into 16 pieces
1/2	cup cilantro, finely chopped
4	cups water (about)
2¼	cups Basmati rice

To prepare:

1. In a large bowl, mix together chicken pieces, garlic, root ginger, chopped green chilies, tomatoes, cumin seeds, 1/2 teaspoon salt, lemon juice and lowfat yogurt.
2. In a large saucepan, heat oil and fry onions, whole green chili, cinnamon, black peppercorns, cumin seeds and cardamoms, stirring frequently, until the onions are soft.
3. Carefully add mixture from the bowl to the saucepan. Mix well, cover and cook for 10 to 15 minutes, stirring occasionally.
4. Add potatoes, 3/4 teaspoon salt, cilantro, and about 4 cups water (enough to make 4½ cups of liquid in all). Stir well, cover saucepan and bring to boil.

Chicken Pilav
Chicken Akni

5. Wash rice, drain and add to the saucepan. Cover saucepan partially, bring to boil and cook for 10 minutes.
6. Reduce heat to low, cover and cook for 10-15 minutes or until the rice is cooked.

Serve with Salads, Pickles, Non-fat yogurt and/or Raita of your choice (page 61).

Please discard whole spices when eating.

Nutrient Analysis (per serving):

Calories	475
Protein	33.9 gm
Carbohydrates	61.6 gm
Total Fat	9.7 gm
Saturated Fat	1.3 gm
Cholesterol	67.5 mg
Sodium with salt included	440.7 mg
Sodium with salt omitted	104.8 mg

Festive Chicken and Rice
Chicken Biryani

For 8 servings you will need:

For Chicken masala:

Ingredients for the marinade:

2½ *pounds chicken breasts, skinned, all visible fat removed and cut into 16 pieces, approx. 5 ounces per serving*
2   *cups tomatoes, fresh or canned without salt, blended*
2   *cups lowfat yogurt*
2   *tablespoons lemon juice*
4   *teaspoons garlic, minced*
4   *teaspoons root ginger, minced*
1/2 *cup onions, finely chopped*
1   *tablespoon canola oil*
3/4 *teaspoon salt (optional)*
1/8 *teaspoon saffron*
1-2 *green chilies, seeded and chopped*
2   *1-inch sticks cinnamon*
2   *whole cardamoms*
2   *whole cloves*

----

1   *pound potatoes, peeled and cut into 16 pieces*
     canola oil for frying onions
2   *cups onions, finely sliced*
2   *teaspoons garam masala*
1/2 *teaspoon red chili powder (optional)*
1/2 *cup tomato paste without salt*

For Saffron Rice:
2½ *cups Basmati rice*
1   *teaspoon salt (optional)*
5   *cups water*
1   *pinch saffron*
1/4 *teaspoon yellow food color*
1   *ounce corn oil margarine*
2   *1-inch sticks cinnamon*
3   *whole cardamoms*
4   *whole cloves*

Festive Chicken and Rice
Chicken Biryani

To prepare:

Chicken masala:
1. In a large bowl, combine all the marinade ingredients and marinate chicken for 4 hours or overnight in a refrigerator.
2. Parboil potatoes, drain and set aside.
3. In a frying pan, heat oil and fry onions until golden brown. Remove onions with a slotted spoon, drain on paper towels.
4. In a large saucepan, cover and cook marinade for 20 minutes.
5. Add garam masala, red chili powder, tomato paste, fried onions and parboiled potatoes. Mix well, cover and cook over low heat for 10 minutes.

Saffron Rice:
1. In a large saucepan, bring 4-3/4 cups water to boil.
2. Wash and drain rice, and add to the boiling water.
3. Add salt, cover saucepan partially and bring to boil again.
4. Cook until almost all the water is absorbed, about 5 to 10 minutes.
5. Reduce heat to low, cover and cook for 10 minutes.
6. In 1/4 cup of water, mix yellow color and saffron, and pour over the rice. Fold the rice gently, cover and cook for 5 minutes or until the rice is done.
7. In a small saucepan, heat margarine. Fry cinnamon, cardamoms and cloves for 1 minute. Pour over the rice and cover immediately. Remove from heat.

Serve Chicken Masala on a bed of Saffron Rice with Salads, Pickles, Chutneys and Raita of your choice (page 61).

Please discard whole spices when eating.

Nutrient Analysis (per serving):

Calories	555
Protein	36.4 gm
Carbohydrates	72.4 gm
Total Fat	13.1 gm
Saturated Fat	2.1 gm
Cholesterol	69.2 mg
Sodium with salt included	642.0 mg
Sodium with salt omitted	171.7 mg

Beef Curry

For 4 servings you will need:

Ingredients for the spice mixture:
3   teaspoons garlic, minced
3   teaspoons root ginger, minced
2   cups tomatoes, fresh or canned without salt, finely chopped
4   tablespoons tomato paste without salt
1/8 teaspoon ground turmeric
4   teaspoons ground coriander
2   teaspoons ground cumin
1   teaspoon garam masala
1/4 teaspoon red chili powder (optional)
1/2 teaspoon salt (optional)

----

2   tablespoons canola oil
1/2 cup onions, quartered and finely sliced
1   pound very lean sirloin, all visible fat removed,
    and cut into 16 cubes, approx 4 ounces per serving
3   cups water
3/4 pounds potatoes, peeled & cut into 12 pieces
1   tablespoon lemon juice
1/4 cup cilantro, chopped

To prepare:

1. In a bowl, assemble all the spice mixture ingredients .
2. In a large saucepan, heat oil and sauté onions until golden
    brown. Discard 1 tablespoon oil.
3. Add spice mixture from the bowl, mix well and cook for 5
    minutes, stirring occasionally.
4. Add beef, mix well, lower heat slightly, cover, and cook for 15
    minutes, stirring occasionally. Add a little water if the
    mixture gets too dry.

Beef Curry

5. Add 3 cups water, mix, cover and bring to boil. Lower heat and simmer for 15 minutes.
6. Add potatoes and cook for 15 minutes, or until potatoes are done. If the curry becomes too thick, add a little water.
7. Add lemon juice, mix, garnish with cilantro and serve.

Serve with bread (page 169) and/or rice (page 163) of your choice, accompanied by Salads, Pickles, Chutneys and Raita of your preference (page 61).

Healthful Tip: Cook this curry in advance, cool, and refrigerate for at least 3 hours or overnight. Skim off all the set fat, reheat and serve.

Nutrient Analysis (per serving):

Calories	305
Protein	28.2 gm
Carbohydrates	27.8 gm
Total Fat	9.7 gm
Saturated Fat	2.2 gm
Cholesterol	69.2 mg
Sodium with salt included	360.6 mg
Sodium with salt omitted	91.9 mg

Lamb Curry

For 4 servings you will need:

Ingredients for the spice mixture:

3   *teaspoons garlic, minced*
3   *teaspoons root ginger, minced*
2   *cups tomatoes, fresh or canned without salt, finely chopped*
4   *tablespoons tomato paste without salt*
1/8 *teaspoon ground turmeric*
4   *teaspoons ground coriander*
2   *teaspoons ground cumin*
1   *teaspoon garam masala*
1/2 *teaspoon salt (optional)*
1/4 *teaspoon red chili powder (optional)*

----

2   *tablespoons canola oil*
1/2 *cup onions, quartered and finely sliced*
1   *pound leg of lamb, all visible fat removed & cut into 16 cubes,*
      approx 4 ounces per serving
3   *cups water*
3/4 *pounds potatoes, peeled & cut into 16 pieces*
1   *tablespoon lemon juice*
1/4 *cup cilantro, chopped*

To prepare:

1.   In a bowl, assemble the spice mixture ingredients.
2.   In a large saucepan, heat oil and sauté onions until golden
     brown. Discard 1 tablespoon oil.
3.   Add spice mixture from the bowl, mix well and cook for 5
     minutes, stirring occasionally.
4.   Add lamb, mix, lower heat slightly, cover and cook for 15
     minutes, stirring occasionally. Add a little water if the
     mixture gets too dry.

Lamb Curry

5. Add 3 cups water, mix, cover, and bring to boil. Lower heat and simmer for 15 minutes.
6. Add potatoes and cook for 15 minutes, or until the potatoes are done. If the curry becomes too dry, add a little water.
7. Add lemon juice, mix, garnish with cilantro and serve.

Serve with bread (page 169) and/or rice (page 163) of your choice, accompanied by Salads, Pickles, Chutneys and Raita of your preference (page 61).

Healthful Tip: Cook this curry in advance, cool, and refrigerate for at least 3 hours or overnight. Skim off any set fat, reheat and serve.

Nutrient Analysis (per serving):

Calories	308
Protein	27.4 gm
Carbohydrates	27.8 gm
Total Fat	10.5 gm
Saturated Fat	2.5 gm
Cholesterol	74.8 mg
Sodium with salt included	367.4 mg
Sodium with salt omitted	98.7 mg

Rice

Please also see:

Plain Rice

For 4 servings you will need:

2½ *cups water*
1/2 *teaspoon salt (optional)*
1¼ *cups Basmati rice*

To prepare:

1. In a large saucepan, bring water to boil.
2. Wash rice, drain and add to the boiling water.
3. Add salt, cover saucepan partially and bring to boil again.
4. Cook for 5 to 10 minutes or until almost all the water is absorbed.
5. Reduce heat to low, cover saucepan and cook for further 10 minutes or until the rice is done.

Nutrient Analysis (per serving):

Calories	211
Protein	4.1 gm
Carbohydrates	46.2 gm
Total Fat	0.4 gm
Saturated Fat	0.1 gm
Cholesterol	0 mg
Sodium with salt included	269.4 mg
Sodium with salt omitted	3.3 mg

Lightly Flavored Rice

For 4 servings you will need:

2   *teaspoons canola oil*
12 *whole black peppercorns*
1/2 *teaspoon whole cumin seeds*
1   *1-inch stick cinnamon*
2½ *cups water*
1/2 *teaspoon salt*
1¼ *cups Basmati rice*

To prepare:

1. In a large saucepan, heat oil and fry peppercorns, cumin and cinnamon for 1/2 minute.
2. Carefully add water and salt, and bring to boil.
3. Wash rice, drain and add to the boiling water.
4. Cover saucepan partially and bring to boil again. Cook for 5 to 10 minutes or until almost all the water is absorbed.
5. Reduce heat to low, cover the saucepan and cook for 10 minutes or until the rice is done.

Please discard whole spices when eating.

Nutrient Analysis (per serving):

Calories	235
Protein	4.3 gm
Carbohydrates	46.9 gm
Total Fat	2.9 gm
Saturated Fat	0.3 gm
Cholesterol	0 mg
Sodium with salt included	270.4 mg
Sodium with salt omitted	3.5 mg

Saffron Rice

For 6 servings you will need:

4   cups water
2   cups Basmati rice
3/4 teaspoon salt (optional)
1/8 teaspoon yellow color
1   pinch saffron
2   tablespoons corn oil margarine
2   1-inch sticks cinnamon
3   whole cardamoms
4   whole cloves

To prepare:

1. In a large saucepan, bring 3-3/4 cups water to boil.
2. Wash rice, drain and add to the boiling water.
3. Add salt, cover saucepan partially and bring to boil again. Cook for 5 to 10 minutes or until almost all the water is absorbed.
4. Reduce heat to low, cover and cook for 8 to 10 minutes.
5. In 1/4 cup of water, mix yellow color and saffron, and pour over the rice and fold in gently. Cover saucepan and cook for 5 minutes or until the rice is done.
6. In a small saucepan, heat margarine and fry cinnamon, cardamoms and cloves for 1 minute. Pour over the rice and cover immediately. Remove from heat and serve.

Serve with curry dishes, Kababs (pages 51, 55, 58), Tandoori Chicken (page 146) and Chicken Tikka (page 54).

Please discard whole spices when eating.

Nutrient Analysis (per serving):

Calories	260
Protein	4.4 gm
Carbohydrates	49.7 gm
Total Fat	4.2 gm
Saturated Fat	0.8 gm
Cholesterol	0 mg
Sodium with salt included	320.6 mg
Sodium with salt omitted	51.6 mg

Rice with Lentil
Chuti Khichdi

For 6 servings you will need:

1   *tablespoon canola oil*
1/2 *teaspoon garlic, minced*
12   *whole black peppercorns*
2   *1-inch sticks cinnamon*
2   *whole cloves*
1/2 *teaspoon cumin seeds*
1/4 *teaspoon ground turmeric*
4   *cups water*
3/4 *teaspoon salt (optional)*
1   *cup masoor or mung daal (split and hulled lentil)*
1   *cup Basmati rice*

To prepare:

1. In a saucepan heat oil and sauté garlic, whole peppercorns, cinnamon, cloves and cumin seeds for 30 seconds.
2. Add turmeric, immediately followed by water and salt, and bring to boil.
3. Wash rice and lentils in water several times. Drain and add to the boiling water. Bring to boil again, cover partially and cook until almost all the water is absorbed; about 10 minutes.
4. Reduce heat to low, cover the saucepan and cook for 15 to 20 minutes, or until the rice and lentils are done.

Serve with Kadhi (page 112) or curry dishes.

Please discard whole spices when eating.

Nutrient Analysis (per serving):

Calories	245
Protein	11.3 gm
Carbohydrates	43.7 gm
Total Fat	2.9 gm
Saturated Fat	0.3 gm
Cholesterol	0 mg
Sodium with salt included	272.1 mg
Sodium with salt omitted	3.7 mg

Creamed Mung Beans and Rice
Lisi Khichdi

For 6 servings you will need:

7   *cups water*
3/4   *teaspoon salt (optional)*
1   *cup mung daal (split mung beans with husk)*
1   *cup long grain rice (Basmati is not ideal)*
1   *tablespoon corn oil margarine*

To prepare:

1.   In a large saucepan, bring 6 cups of water to boil.
2.   Wash mung daal and rice in water several times. Drain and add to the boiling water.
3.   Add salt, cover partially, bring to boil, and cook for 10 minutes.
4.   Reduce heat slightly, cover and cook for further 15 to 20 minutes, or until rice and mung beans are tender.
5.   Add 1 cup of water, cover and cook over very low heat until the mung and rice are very soft, about 10 minutes.
6.   Remove from heat, add margarine and mix thoroughly (cream) with a wooden spoon to a near-smooth consistency.

Serve with vegetable and meat curries, Kadhi (page 112), nonfat milk, or nonfat yogurt.

Nutrient Analysis (per serving):

Calories	249
Protein	10.4 gm
Carbohydrates	46.3 gm
Total Fat	2.5 gm
Saturated Fat	0.5 gm
Cholesterol	0 mg
Sodium with salt included	289.8 mg
Sodium with salt omitted	21.1 mg

Breads

Indian Whole-Wheat Bread
Chapati

For 8 Chapatis you will need:

1½ *cups whole wheat flour*
1/2 *cup oat bran*
1   *tablespoon canola oil*
     water
     all-purpose flour for dusting

To prepare:

1. Preheat griddle.
2. In a large bowl, mix flour and oat bran. Make a well in the center, add oil and make a crumbly mixture with fingertips.
3. Gradually add water (a shade under 3/4 cup) and make a pliable dough and knead well until smooth. (See page 235).
4. Divide dough into 8 equal portions and shape into balls.
5. Roll out each ball into a 3-inch (8 cm) round. Smear top surface very lightly with oil and sprinkle lightly with flour.
6. Gather up the edges of the round, bring to the center and pinch together so that the round now looks like an onion.
7. Turn over, flatten slightly and roll into a 6-inch (15 cm) flat round, lightly dusting with flour as necessary.
8. Cook on a pre-heated griddle, top side first until lightly mottled; about 10 to 15 seconds. Turn over and cook for about 45 seconds. Turn over again and cook for about 30 seconds or until cooked. Place Chapati on a plate, down side up.
9. Repeat the process to make the remaining Chapatis. Stack and cover until ready to serve.

Serve with any curry dish, or with fruit preserves.

Nutrient Analysis (per serving):

Calories	106
Protein	4.1 gm
Carbohydrates	20.2 gm
Total Fat	2.6 gm
Saturated Fat	0.3 gm
Cholesterol	0 mg
Sodium	1.4 mg

Pan "Fried" Whole-Wheat Bread
Paratha

For 8 Paratha you will need:

1½   *cups whole wheat flour*
1/2   *cup oat bran*
1/4   *teaspoon salt (optional)*
6   *teaspoons canola oil*
      water
      all-purpose flour for dusting

To prepare:

1. Preheat griddle.
2. In a large bowl,mix flour, oat bran and salt.
3. Make a well in the center, add 2 teaspoons oil and make a crumbly mixture with fingertips..
4. Gradually add water (a shade under 3/4 cup) and make a pliable dough and knead until smooth. (See page 235).
5. Divide dough into 8 equal portions and shape into balls. Flatten slightly and roll out into 5-inch (13 cm) flat rounds, lightly dusting with flour as necessary.
6. Cook each round on the pre-heated griddle, top side first, for 15 seconds. Turn over and cook for about 45 seconds. Place on a plate and smear each side with 1/4 teaspoon of oil.
7. Cook remaining rounds as above and stack on the plate. Keep covered until ready to 'fry'.
8. Heat a nonstick skillet and 'dry fry' the rounds, one at a time, for 20 to 30 seconds on each side. Stack the Paratha on a plate and cover until ready to serve.

Serve hot or cold with any curry dish, or with fruit preserves.

Nutrient Analysis (per Paratha):

Calories	122
Protein	4.1 gm
Carbohydrates	20.2 gm
Total Fat	4.3 gm
Saturated Fat	0.4 gm
Cholesterol	0 mg
Sodium with salt included	68.0 mg
Sodium with salt omitted	1.4 mg

Pan "Fried" Whole wheat Savory Bread
Savory Paratha

For 8 Paratha you will need:

1½ *cups whole wheat flour*
1/2 *cup oat bran*
1   *teaspoon garlic, minced*
1   *teaspoon ginger, minced*
1   *teaspoon green chili, seeded and minced*
1/4 *cup cilantro, minced*
1/4 *teaspoon salt (optional)*
1/4 *teaspoon ground turmeric*
1   *teaspoon ground cumin*
6   *teaspoons canola oil*
     water
     all-purpose flour for dusting

To prepare:

1. Preheat a griddle.
2. In a large bowl, mix flour, oat bran, garlic, ginger, green chili, cilantro, salt, turmeric, and cumin.
3. Make a well in the center, add 2 teaspoons oil and make a crumbly mixture with fingertips..
4. Gradually add water (a shade under 3/4 cup) and make a pliable dough; knead until smooth. (See page 235).
5. Divide dough into 8 equal portions and shape into balls. Flatten slightly and roll out into 5-inch (13 cm) flat rounds, lightly dusting with flour as necessary.
6. Cook each round on the pre-heated griddle, top side first for 15 seconds. Turn over and cook for about 45 seconds. Place on a plate and smear each side with 1/4 teaspoon of oil.
7. Cook remaining rounds as above and stack on the plate. Keep covered until ready to 'fry'.
8. Heat a nonstick skillet and 'dry fry' the rounds, one at a time, for 20 to 30 seconds on each side. Stack the Paratha on a plate and cover until ready to serve.

Pan "Fried" Whole wheat Savory Bread
Savory Paratha

Serve with curries, Pickles, Chutneys and Raita of your choice (page 61) and/or a cup of hot tea or nonfat milk.

Nutrient Analysis (per serving):

Calories	128
Protein	4.4 gm
Carbohydrates	21.5 gm
Total Fat	4.4 gm
Saturated Fat	0.4 gm
Cholesterol	0 mg
Sodium with salt included	69.4 mg
Sodium with salt omitted	2.2 mg

Leavened Bread
Naan

For 5 Naan you will need:

1½ teaspoons all-purpose flour
1/2 teaspoon sugar
1/4 cup warm water, about 110° F*
1/2 teaspoon rapid-rise yeast

1½ cups all-purpose flour
1/4 teaspoon salt (optional)
1/2 teaspoon baking powder, low sodium
    warm water

To prepare:

1. In a jug, combine 1½ teaspoons all-purpose flour, sugar and
    warm water. Add yeast, stir, cover and let stand for 5
    minutes, or until frothy on the top.
2. In a large bowl, combine flour, salt and baking powder. Make
    a well in the center and pour in the yeast mixture. Gradually
    add warm water and make an elastic but not sticky dough
    (see page 235).
3. Put the dough on a lightly floured surface and knead for 7 to
    8 minutes until smooth.
4. Shape into a ball and return to the bowl. Cover bowl with
    plastic wrap and a clean towel. Keep in a warm place for 1
    hour to rise.
5. Punch dough for 2 minutes, cover and leave for 20 minutes to
    rise again.
6. Preheat broiler and heat a griddle.
7. Divide dough into 5 equal portions and roll into 6-inch
    (15 cm) rounds on a lightly floured surface. Keep unrolled
    portions covered to prevent from drying.
8. Bake on hot griddle, top side down, for about 30 seconds or
    until bubbles appear on top and the underside is mottled.
9. Lift with a spatula and place on a baking sheet, uncooked side
    up. Broil for 30 seconds or until the Naan puffs up and is
    cooked.

Leavened Bread
Naan

Serve with curry dishes, Kababs (pages 51, 55, 58), Tandoori
Chicken (page 146) and Chicken Tikka (page 54). Also make
Naan pocket sandwiches.

* Note: Water at 110° F temperature is just hot enough to hold
your little finger in it without burning.

Nutrient Analysis (per serving):

Calories	140
Protein	4.1 gm
Carbohydrates	29.3 gm
Total Fat	0.4 gm
Saturated Fat	0.1 gm
Cholesterol	0 mg
Sodium with salt included	107.6 mg
Sodium with salt omitted	0.1 mg

Leavened Whole-wheat Bread
Whole-wheat Naan

For 6 Naan you will need:

1   *teaspoon sugar*
3/4   *cup warm water, about 110° F**
1   *envelope rapid-rise dry yeast*
1½   *cups whole wheat flour*
3/4   *cup all-purpose flour*
1/4   *teaspoon salt (optional)*

To prepare:

1.   In a jug, combine sugar and warm water. Add yeast, stir and let stand for 5 minutes until frothy on the top.
2.   In a large bowl, mix both the flours and salt . Make a well in the center, pour in the yeast mixture and make dough.
3.   Knead the dough on a lightly floured surface for 7 to 8 minutes until smooth. (See page 235).
4.   Shape dough into a ball and return to the bowl. Cover the bowl with plastic wrap and a clean towel. Keep in a warm place for 30 minutes to rise.
5.   Preheat broiler and heat a griddle.
6.   Punch and knead dough for 2 minutes. Divide into 6 equal portions and roll into 7-inch (18 cm) rounds on a lightly floured surface. Keep unrolled portions covered.
7.   Bake on hot griddle, top side down, for about 30 seconds or until little bubbles appear on the top and the underside is mottled.
8.   Lift with a spatula and place on a baking sheet, uncooked side up. Broil for 30 seconds or until the Naan puffs up and is cooked.

Serve with curry dishes, Tandoori Chicken and Chicken Tikka.

Nutrient Analysis (per Naan):

Calories	164
Protein	6.2 gm
Carbohydrates	34.8 gm
Total Fat	0.7 gm
Saturated Fat	0.1 gm
Cholesterol	0 mg
Sodium with salt included	91.3 mg
Sodium with salt omitted	1.7 mg

Deep-fried Whole-wheat Bread
Poori

For 24 Poori you will need:

1½ *cups whole wheat flour*
1/2 *cup oat bran*
1 *tablespoon canola oil*
   water
   all-purpose flour for dusting
   canola oil for frying

To prepare:

1. In a large bowl, combine flour and oat bran.
2. Make a well in the center, add oil and make a crumbly mixture with fingertips. Gradually add water (a shade under 3/4 cup) to make a pliable dough; knead until smooth. See page 235).
3. Divide dough into 24 equal portions and shape into balls. Roll out into rounds, about 3 inches (8 cm) in diameter, lightly dusting with flour as necessary.
4. In a deep frying pan, heat oil. Place each round (Poori) in hot oil, top side down, and deep fry. Press gently with a slotted spoon to encourage Poori to puff up. Turn over and fry until light beige, about 10 seconds.
5. Remove with slotted spoon, drain on paper towel and serve.

Serve with curries, Pickles, Chutneys and Raita of your choice (page 61) and/or a cup of hot tea or nonfat milk.

Author's Note: Deep fried foods are recommended for occasional eating only, even though they are made of healthful ingredients.

Nutrient Analysis (per serving):

Calories	56
Protein	1.4 gm
Carbohydrates	6.7 gm
Total Fat	3.2 gm
Saturated Fat	0.3 gm
Cholesterol	0 mg
Sodium	0.5 mg

Millet Flour Bread
Rotlo

For 1 bread (8 servings) you will need:

1   cup millet flour
2   tablespoons whole wheat flour
    water
1   tablespoon canola or corn oil margarine (optional)

To prepare:

1.   Preheat griddle.
2.   In a large bowl, sieve millet flour. Add whole wheat flour and mix. Make a well in the center and gradually add water and make a firm smooth dough. Knead for 2 minutes. (see p 235)
3.   Wet palms of your hands and shape the dough into a smooth ball. Flatten the ball slightly and place it on a 12-inch square piece of grease-proof paper. Place a 12-inch square piece of plastic wrap over it and very gently roll into an 8-inch (20 cm) diameter round of even thickness. Remove the plastic wrap.
4.   Lift the paper with the round on it, slap the round on the pre-heated griddle, top side down, and remove the paper. Reduce heat and cook for 2 minutes or until the underside is mottled.
5.   Slip a spatula under the round to loosen, carefully lift and turn over, and cook for 4 to 5 minutes.
6.   Carefully lift and turn over the round once again and let it cook over a very low heat for 5 to 7 minutes.
7.   Carefully lift and turn the Rotlo over onto a serving plate, down side up.
8.   Spread margarine evenly on the Rotlo and serve.

Serve with vegetable curries, fish curries, Kadhi (page 112) and nonfat yogurt.

Nutrient Analysis (per serving):

Calories	119
Protein	3.3 gm
Carbohydrates	20.8 gm
Total Fat	2.5 gm
Saturated Fat	0.4 gm
Cholesterol	0 mg
Sodium	20.4 mg

Fat-free Whole-wheat Savory Pancakes
Dosa

For 8 Dosa you will need:

1   *cup whole wheat flour*
2   *tablespoons gram (chickpea) flour*
1/4   *teaspoon salt (optional)*
1/4   *teaspoon turmeric*
1/4   *cup cilantro, minced*
1   *green chili, seeded and minced (optional)*
1¼   *cups lukewarm water*

To prepare:

1. In a large bowl, combine whole-wheat flour, gram flour, salt, turmeric, cilantro and green chili. Make a well in the center, gradually add water and make a smooth batter. Cover and set aside for 30 minutes.
2. Beat the batter for 2 minutes.
3. Heat an 8-inch (20 cm) nonstick skillet. Pour a ladleful of batter (4 tablespoons) and quickly tilt the pan in all directions so that the batter covers the base of the pan.
4. Cook for 1 to 2 minutes or until the underside is mottled. Carefully turn over with a spatula and cook for 1 minute, or until cooked through.
5. Repeat the process with the remaining batter, stack Dosa on a plate, and cover until ready to serve.

Serve hot with Sambar (page 110), any dry vegetable curry or nonfat yogurt.

Nutrient Analysis (per serving):

Calories	65
Protein	2.8 gm
Carbohydrates	13.4 gm
Total Fat	0.5 gm
Saturated Fat	0.1 gm
Cholesterol	0 mg
Sodium with salt included	68.7 mg
Sodium with salt omitted	1.5 mg

Fat-free Rice and Lentil Cakes
Idli

For 2 cakes (12 slices) you will need:

1/2 cup urad daal, (split and hulled black mung)
1¼ cup hot water
1 cup rice flour
1/4 teaspoon salt (optional)
1¼ teaspoon baking soda

To prepare:

1. Sort, wash and soak urad daal in cold water for 4 to 5 hours or overnight. Drain, rinse and drain.
2. In a blender, process daal and 1/4 cup water to a smooth creamy mixture. Transfer the mixture to a bowl.
3. Add rice flour and remaining water and mix to a smooth batter. Leave to marinate for 30 minutes.
4. Prepare a steamer.
5. Add salt and baking soda to the batter and mix well. Pour the batter into two 8-inch (20 cm) round nonstick cake pans* and steam for 20 to 25 minutes. Test with a wooden toothpick. If it comes out clean, the Idli is ready. Cut into 12 slices and serve.

* To make individual Idlis, pour mixture into a 12-cup or two 6-cup muffin trays and steam as in Step 5.

Serve Idli with Sambar (page 110) or any curry dish.

Nutrient Analysis (per slice):

Calories	75
Protein	3.0 gm
Carbohydrates	15.1 gm
Total Fat	0.3 gm
Saturated Fat	0.1 gm
Cholesterol	0 mg
Sodium with salt included	164.6 mg
Sodium with salt omitted	78.6 mg

Desserts and Sweets

Royal "Sour Cream" Dessert *(Shrikhand)**   182

Cream of Wheat Halwa *(Seero)**   183

Nonfat-milk Balls in Light Saffron Syrup *(Gulab Jamun)** 184

Bulgar Sweet *(Lapsi)**   186

Sweet Saffron Rice *(Zarda)**   187

Vermicelli Dessert *(Sevian)**   188

Vermicelli Pudding *(Kheer Sevian)*   190

Crêpes *(Chilla)*   191

Carrot Halwa *   192

Indian Milk Junket *(Faludo)*   193

Nonfat Saffron "Ice Cream" *(Nonfat Kesar Kulfi)*   194

Indian Shortbread *(Nankhatai)*   195

Sweet Whole-wheat Fried Bread *(Thepla)*   196

Tropical Fruit Salad   198

Dishes marked with an * can also be served as sweet starters.

Royal 'Sour Cream' Dessert
Shrikhand

For 4 servings you will need:

1   recipe Nonfat *'sour cream'* (see page 226)
2   *tablespoons sugar*
1/4 *teaspoon citric acid (optional)*
1   *pinch saffron*
1/4 *teaspoon cardamom seeds, crushed*
1/4 *teaspoon nutmeg, grated*
1/2 *tablespoon almonds, sliced*
1/2 *tablespoon pistachios, sliced*

To prepare:

1.   In a bowl, combine 'sour cream,' sugar, and citric acid. Beat
     to a smooth consistency.
2.   Add cardamoms, nutmeg and saffron, mix well and chill.
3.   Garnish with sliced almonds and pistachio before serving.

Serve with Chapati (page 170) or Poori (page 177) as an hors
d'oeuvre, or on it own as a dessert.

Nutrient Analysis (per serving):

Calories	172
Protein	13.8 gm
Carbohydrates	24.3 gm
Total Fat	2.3 gm
Saturated Fat	0.5 gm
Cholesterol	4.1 mg
Sodium	174.0 mg

Cream of Wheat Halwa
Seero

For 10 servings you will need:

2   *ounces corn oil margarine*
1   *cup cream of wheat (regular)*
1/4   *cup golden raisins*
3   *cups nonfat milk*
1/4   *cup nonfat dry milk powder*
1/2   *cup sugar*
1/8   *teaspoon saffron*
1/8   *teaspoon yellow color*
1/2   *teaspoon nutmeg, grated*
1/2   *teaspoon cardamom seeds, crushed*
1/2   *tablespoon almonds, finely sliced*
1/2   *tablespoon pistachio, finely sliced*

To prepare:

1. In a large saucepan, melt margarine, and sauté cream of wheat over medium heat, stirring continuously, until light golden in color; about 10 minutes.
2. Add raisins and continue cooking, stirring all the time, until the raisins are swollen.
3. Remove the saucepan from heat. Carefully add nonfat milk and stir well.
4. Return the saucepan to heat, add dry milk, sugar, saffron, color, nutmeg and cardamoms and mix. Bring to boil and cook, stirring continuously, until the mixture thickens and begins to leave the side of the saucepan.
5. Reduce heat to very low, cover the saucepan and cook for further 5 minutes.
6. Serve garnished with sliced almonds and pistachios.

Nutrient Analysis (per serving):

Calories	200
Protein	5.9 gm
Carbohydrates	31.6 gm
Total Fat	5.8 gm
Saturated Fat	1.0 gm
Cholesterol	1.8 mg
Sodium	116.3 mg

Nonfat-milk Balls in Light Saffron Syrup
Gulab Jamun

For 24 Gulab Jamun you will need:

For syrup:

3	*cups water*
1¼	*cups sugar*
1	*pinch saffron*
1/4	*teaspoon yellow food color*

For milk balls:

1	*cup nonfat dry milk powder*
6	*tablespoons cream of wheat (regular)*
6	*tablespoons all purpose flour*
1	*teaspoon baking powder*
1/4	*teaspoon nutmeg, grated*
1/4	*teaspoon cardamoms seeds, crushed*
1/8	*teaspoon saffron*
2	*ounces corn oil margarine*
1/2	*cup nonfat milk for binding*
	canola oil for frying

To prepare:

1. In a heavy-bottomed saucepan, bring water, sugar, saffron and food color to boil. Reduce heat and simmer for 10 to 15 minutes. Remove saucepan from heat.
2. In a large bowl, combine nonfat milk powder, cream of wheat, flour, baking powder, nutmeg, cardamoms and saffron.
3. Add margarine and rub in with fingertips until the mixture looks like fine bread crumbs.
4. Slowly add nonfat milk (about 1/2 cup), make a soft dough, and let stand for 30 minutes.
5. Lightly oil palms of your hands with canola oil, take a spoonful of dough at a time and shape into 24 round balls.

Nonfat-milk Balls in
Light Saffron Syrup
Gulab Jamun

6.   In a deep frying pan, heat oil and deep fry milk balls over a
     gentle heat . The balls will swell and turn over by themselves.
     Fry until golden brown. (If milk balls do not turn over by
     themselves, gently turn them with a spoon.)
7.   Lift with a perforated spoon and drain on paper towels.
8.   Place Gulab Jamun (milk balls) in a serving bowl and pour
     warm syrup over them and soak for at least 30 minutes.

Serve warm or cold.

Author's Note: Deep-fried foods are recommended for occasional
eating only, even though they are made of healthful ingredients.

Nutrient Analysis (per Gulab Jamun):

Calories	105
Protein	1.9 gm
Carbohydrates	15.7 gm
Total Fat	4.0 gm
Saturated Fat	0.5 gm
Cholesterol	0.7 mg
Sodium	57.2 mg

Bulgar Sweet
Lapsi

For 10 servings you will need:

1   *ounce corn oil margarine*
1¼ *cups coarsely ground wheat (Bulgar)*
1   *tablespoon fennel seeds*
1/4 *cup golden raisins, seedless*
2¼ *cups nonfat milk*
1/4 *cup nonfat dry milk powder*
1/2 *cup sugar (reduce if preferred)*
1   *pinch saffron*
1/4 *teaspoon yellow food color*
1/2 *teaspoon cardamoms, crushed*
1/2 *teaspoon nutmeg, grated*
2   *tablespoons almonds, finely sliced*

To prepare:

1. In a saucepan, heat margarine and sauté wheat and fennel seeds, stirring frequently, until the wheat is light golden brown; about 10 to 15 minutes. Add raisins and cook until the raisins are swollen. Remove saucepan from heat.
2. Carefully add nonfat milk, nonfat milk powder, sugar, saffron, and yellow food color. Stir well, and bring to boil.
3. Reduce heat slightly, cover and cook until almost all the liquid has been absorbed.
4. Add cardamoms, nutmeg and fold in. Cover and cook on a very low heat for 20 minutes or until the wheat is cooked but still moist. (Add a little water if too dry.)
5. Garnish with almonds and serve.

Serve as a first course with Pakora (page 38) or Kababs (page 45) and Carrot Pickle (page 68), as a cereal with hot nonfat milk or on its own as a dessert.

Nutrient Analysis (per serving):

Calories	181
Protein	5.7 gm
Carbohydrates	31.1 gm
Total Fat	4.3 gm
Saturated Fat	0.7 gm
Cholesterol	1.5 mg
Sodium	75.0 mg

Sweet Saffron Rice
Zarda

For 10 servings you will need:

3   *ounces corn oil margarine*
6   *whole cardamoms*
2   *1-inch sticks cinnamon*
6   *whole cloves*
1/2 *cup golden raisins, seedless*
4   *cups water*
3/4 *cup sugar*
1/4 *teaspoon saffron*
1/2 *teaspoon yellow food color*
1/2 *teaspoon vanilla extract*
2   *cups Basmati rice*
1   *tablespoon sliced almonds*

To prepare:

1. In a heavy bottomed saucepan, heat margarine and fry cardamoms, cinnamon, cloves and raisins, stirring frequently, until the raisins are swollen.
2. Carefully add water, sugar, saffron, yellow food color and vanilla. Cover and bring to boil.
3. Wash and drain rice and add to the boiling water. Bring to boil again, cover partially and cook for 5 minutes.
4. Reduce heat to slow boiling point, cover and cook for 10 minutes or until most of the water is absorbed.
5. Reduce heat to very low and cook for further 15 to 20 minutes until the rice is done.
6. Garnish with almonds and serve.

Zarda makes a delicious dessert on its own. Traditionally it is also served as a main course with Daal accompanied by Pickles.

Nutrient Analysis (per serving):

Calories	283
Protein	3.1 gm
Carbohydrates	51.1 gm
Total Fat	7.5 gm
Saturated Fat	1.3 gm
Cholesterol	0 mg
Sodium	95.1 mg

Vermicelli Dessert
Sevian

For 10 servings you will need:

4   ounces corn oil margarine
2   1-inch sticks cinnamon
3   whole cardamoms
12 ounces vermicelli, without eggs, broken
1/4 cup golden raisins, seedless
4   cups water
1   cup sugar
1/8 teaspoon saffron
1/2 teaspoon yellow food color
1   teaspoon vanilla extract
1   tablespoon almonds, sliced

To prepare:

1. In a saucepan, heat margarine and sauté cinnamon,
    cardamoms and broken vermicelli, turning frequently with a
    wooden spoon, until vermicelli begins to brown.
2. Add raisins and continue to sauté until vermicelli is evenly
    light golden brown and raisins are swollen.
3. Remove saucepan from heat and discard 3 tablespoons
    margarine. Carefully add water, sugar, saffron, color and
    vanilla extract. Return saucepan to heat and bring to boil.
    Reduce heat, cover and cook until almost all the liquid is
    absorbed.
4. Stir gently, cover, reduce heat to very low and cook for
    further 10 minutes or until the vermicelli is cooked, but moist.
    If it is too dry, add a little water and cook for 1 to 2 minutes.
5. Garnish with almonds and serve.

Vermicelli Dessert
Sevian

Serve as a first course with Pakora (page 38) or Kababs (page 45), accompanied by Carrot Pickle (page 68), **or** on its own as a dessert. Sevian makes an excellent cereal served with hot nonfat milk.

Please discard whole spices when eating.

Nutrient Analysis (per serving):

Calories	275
Protein	4.8 gm
Carbohydrates	48.7 gm
Total Fat	7.0 gm
Saturated Fat	1.2 gm
Cholesterol	0 mg
Sodium	79.6 mg

Vermicelli Pudding
Kheer Sevian

For 4 servings you will need:

4	cups nonfat milk
1/4	cup nonfat dry milk powder
1	tablespoon sugar
1/2	teaspoon cardamoms, crushed
1/2	teaspoon nutmeg, grated
1/8	teaspoon saffron
1	ounce corn oil margarine
3	ounces vermicelli, broken
2	1-inch sticks cinnamon
4	whole cloves
1/2	tablespoon almonds, finely sliced
1/2	tablespoon pistachios, finely sliced

To prepare:

1. In a heavy-bottomed saucepan, combine milk, milk powder, sugar, cardamoms, nutmeg, saffron, almonds and pistachios and bring to boil, stirring continuously.
2. Reduce heat and simmer for 5 minutes, stirring frequently.
3. In another saucepan, melt margarine and sauté cinnamon, cloves and vermicelli, turning frequently with a wooden spoon, until vermicelli is light golden brown. Remove and drain on paper towel.
4. Add drained vermicelli and whole spices to the milk, stir gently, cover partially and simmer for 15 to 20 minutes or until vermicelli is cooked. Stir occasionally to prevent sticking or burning. If Kheer gets too thick, add a little water.

Serve as a dessert on its own, or as a starter with Paratha or Poori. Please discard cinnamon and cloves when eating.

Nutrient Analysis (per serving):

Calories	240
Protein	13.2 gm
Carbohydrates	34.1 gm
Total Fat	5.6 gm
Saturated Fat	1.2 gm
Cholesterol	5.3 mg
Sodium	203.1 mg

Crêpes
Chilla

For 8 crepes you will need:

1   *cup all-purpose flour*
1¼ *cups water*
2   *egg whites*
2   *teaspoons canola oil*
     vegetable oil spray

To prepare:

1. In a large bowl, sift flour. Slowly add water and mix to make a smooth batter.
2. Add egg whites and 2 teaspoons oil, and whisk for 1 minute.
3. Heat an 8- or 9-inch (20 or 23 cm) frying pan, lightly spray with vegetable oil spray and pour a ladleful (4½ tablespoons) of batter. Quickly cover the base of the pan by tilting the pan in all directions.
4. Cook for 30 seconds or until bubbles appear on top and the underside is mottled.
5. Turn over with a spatula and cook for 30 to 40 seconds, or until cooked through. Slide onto a plate.
6. Repeat the process with the remaining batter and stack crêpes on the plate. Cover until ready to serve.

Serve Crêpes hot, sprinkled lightly with sugar and lemon juice, or with fruit preserves.

Nutrient Analysis (per serving):

Calories	79
Protein	2.5 gm
Carbohydrates	12.0 gm
Total Fat	2.2 gm
Saturated Fat	0.2 gm
Cholesterol	0 mg
Sodium	14.0 mg

Carrot Halwa

For 6 servings you will need:

1   *ounce corn oil margarine*
1   *pound carrots, peeled and finely grated*
1½ *cups nonfat milk*
1/2 *cup nonfat dry milk powder*
1/4 *cup golden raisins*
1/8 *teaspoon saffron*
1/2 *teaspoon cardamoms, crushed*
1/2 *teaspoon nutmeg, grated*
1/4 *cup sugar*
1   *tablespoon almonds, slivered*

To prepare:

1. In a saucepan, melt margarine, and cook carrots for 5 minutes, stirring frequently.
2. Add milk and milk powder, bring to boil, reduce heat slightly and cook for 25 minutes, stirring frequently.
3. Add raisins, saffron, cardamoms and nutmeg. Mix well and cook, stirring occasionally, until almost all the liquid has evaporated.
4. Add sugar, mix well, reduce heat to low and cook, stirring occasionally, until the mixture thickens; about 10 to 15 minutes.
5. Pour into a 7-inch (18 cm) round serving dish, garnish with almonds and serve.

Serve hot or cold. Carrot Halwa is a rich exotic dessert which can also be served as a starter.

Nutrient Analysis (per serving):

Calories	175
Protein	5.8 gm
Carbohydrates	27.5 gm
Total Fat	5.4 gm
Saturated Fat	0.9 gm
Cholesterol	2.3 mg
Sodium	143.0 mg

Indian Milk Junket
Faludo

For 8 servings you will need:

1/2   *cup Agar Agar (Chinese grass), 1/3 ounce*
1   *cup water*
5   *cups nonfat milk*
1   *cup nonfat dry milk powder*
2½ *tablespoons sugar*
1/2 *teaspoon vanilla extract*
1/4 *teaspoon red food color*
1/4 *teaspoon cardamom seeds, freshly ground*
1/4 *teaspoon nutmeg, freshly grated*

To prepare:

1. Rinse and soak Agar-Agar in cold water for 15 minutes. Drain.
2. In a heavy-bottomed saucepan, boil Agar-Agar in water, over medium heat, until completely dissolved.
3. In the meantime, in another heavy-bottomed saucepan, combine milk, dry milk powder and sugar. Slowly bring to boil, stirring continuously. Reduce heat and simmer for 2 minutes, stirring continuously.
4. Gradually pour the milk into the dissolved and simmering Agar-Agar, stirring continuously. Add vanilla extract, color, cardamoms and nutmeg. Bring to boil and cook for 5 minutes, stirring continuously.
5. Strain into 8 individual serving bowls and leave to set. When cool, cover and refrigerate until ready to serve. Serve cold.

Variation: Use a pinch of saffron instead of vanilla extract.

Nutrient Analysis (per serving):

Calories	106
Protein	8.6 gm
Carbohydrates	17.0 gm
Total Fat	0.4 gm
Saturated Fat	0.2 gm
Cholesterol	4.5 mg
Sodium	123.3 mg

Nonfat Saffron "Ice Cream"
Nonfat Kesar Kulfi

For 6 servings you will need:

2   *tablespoons corn flour or corn starch*
2   *tablespoons sugar*
2   *cups nonfat milk*
1   *cup nonfat dry milk powder*
1   *teaspoon vanilla extract*
1/4 *teaspoon cardamom seeds, freshly crushed*
1/4 *teaspoon nutmeg, freshly grated*
1/8 *teaspoon saffron*

To prepare:

1. In a large oven-proof bowl, combine and mix corn flour, sugar and 2 tablespoons nonfat milk into a smooth mixture.
2. In a heavy-bottomed saucepan, slowly bring to boil the remaining nonfat milk, nonfat dry milk powder, vanilla, cardamom seeds, nutmeg and saffron, stirring continuously.
3. Gradually pour the hot milk into the bowl with corn flour mixture, stirring continuously in order to prevent lumps.
4. Pour the mixture back into the saucepan and bring to boil, stirring continuously. Remove from heat and allow to cool.
5. Pour into a suitable container for freezing. Cover securely with foil and place in the coldest part of a freezer for 30 to 45 minutes or until 1/2 inch of Kulfi is frozen around the sides.
6. Whisk for 2 minutes. Cover and return to the freezer for 20 to 25 minutes. Whisk again for 2 minutes, pour into one large or 6 individual ice cream containers, cover and return to the freezer.

Kulfi is harder than regular ice cream. Therefore, transfer to the refrigerator for 1 hour before serving.

Nutrient Analysis (per serving):

Calories	98
Protein	7.4 gm
Carbohydrates	16.2 gm
Total Fat	0.3 gm
Saturated Fat	0.2 gm
Cholesterol	3.8 mg
Sodium	106.9 mg

Indian Shortbread
Nankhatai

For 24 servings you will need:

1/2	cup sugar
3	ounces corn oil margarine
1/2	cup cream of wheat (semolina)
3	egg whites
1½	cups all-purpose flour
1	teaspoon baking powder, low sodium
1/8	teaspoon saffron
1	teaspoon vanilla extract
1/2	teaspoon freshly ground nutmeg
1/2	teaspoon ground cardamom
	canola oil
	vegetable oil spray

To prepare:

1. Preheat oven to 350° F.
2. Beat sugar, margarine and egg whites until creamy and soft.
3. Add cream of wheat and beat until creamy.
4. Add flour, baking powder, saffron, vanilla extract, nutmeg and cardamoms, and mix until smooth. Set aside for 15 minutes.
5. Lightly oil palms of your hands with canola oil, take a spoonful of dough at a time and shape into 24 balls.
6. Flatten balls slightly and place 1½ inches apart on a baking sheet lightly sprayed with vegetable oil spray.
7. Bake in the preheated oven for 15 to 20 minutes.

Variation: Use 2 cups of all-purpose flour instead of 1½ cups of flour and 1/2 cup of cream of wheat.

Nutrient Analysis (per serving):

Calories	87
Protein	1.7 gm
Carbohydrates	13.1 gm
Total Fat	3.1 gm
Saturated Fat	0.5 gm
Cholesterol	0 mg
Sodium	45.6 mg

Sweet Whole-wheat Fried Bread
Thepla

For 24 Thepla you will need:

3/4 *cup water*
1/4 *pound jaggery, (2/3 cup tightly packed small pieces)*
2 *cups whole wheat flour*
1 *tablespoon canola oil*
   all-purpose flour for dusting
   canola oil for frying

To prepare:

1. In a saucepan, bring water and jaggery to boil. Cook for 1 minute to soften jaggery. Remove from heat and break up jaggery pieces with the back of a spoon until completely dissolved. Strain.
2. In a large bowl, add flour, make a well in the center, add 1 tablespoon oil and make a crumbly mixture with fingertips.
3. Gradually add warm jaggery water (a shade under 3/4 cup) to make a pliable dough. Sprinkle lightly with all-purpose flour and knead for one minute (see page 235).
4. Divide into 24 equal portions. Roll out each portion into a 3-inch (7.5 cm) diameter round, dusting lightly with flour as necessary. (Keep the unrolled portions covered with plastic wrap to prevent drying).
5. In a deep frying pan, heat oil. Place each round (Thepla) in hot oil top side down and deep fry. Press each Thepla gently with a slotted spoon to encourage it to puff up. Turn over the Thepla and fry until brown.
6. Remove, drain on paper towel and serve.

Sweet Whole-wheat Fried Bread
Thepla

Store Thepla between paper towels, to soak up extra oil, until ready to serve (page 270).

Thepla make excellent snack food. Serve with hot tea or nonfat milk.

Author's Note: Deep fried foods are recommended for occasional eating only, even though they are made of healthful ingredients.

Nutrient Analysis (per Thepla):

Calories	83
Protein	1.4 gm
Carbohydrates	13.2 gm
Total Fat	3.1 gm
Saturated Fat	0.2 gm
Cholesterol	0 mg
Sodium	13.2 mg

Tropical Fruit Salad

For 20 servings you will need:

2   *cups ripe mangos, peeled and cubed*
2   *cups ripe papaya, peeled, seeded and cubed*
1   *cup kiwi fruit, peeled and sliced*
4   *passion fruits*
1   *cup pineapple chunks, canned in juice, drained*
1   *20-ounce can jackfruit, drained*
1   *20-ounce can guava, drained*
1   *20-ounce can mandarin oranges in light syrup*
1   *20-ounce can lychees in light syrup*

To prepare:

1. In a large serving bowl, assemble mangos, papaya, kiwi fruit, flesh of passion fruit, drained pineapple, jackfruit and guava. Mix well.
2. Add mandarin oranges and lychees along with their syrup and mix gently.
3. Chill until ready to serve.

Serve cold on its own. Tropical Fruit Salad makes a delightfully refreshing dessert after a spicy meal.

Nutrient Analysis (per serving):

Calories	90
Protein	0.9 gm
Carbohydrates	23.2 gm
Total Fat	0.3 gm
Saturated Fat	0 gm
Cholesterol	0 mg
Sodium	9.2 mg

Drinks

Festive Saffron Milk
Kadho

For 8 servings you will need:

8   *cups nonfat milk*
1/2 *cup nonfat dry milk powder*
1/8 *teaspoon saffron*
1/4 *teaspoon ground cardamoms*
1/4 *teaspoon ground nutmeg*
8   *teaspoons sugar*
3   *tablespoons almonds, coarsely ground*
2   *tablespoons pistachio, coarsely ground*

To prepare:

1. In a large, heavy-bottomed saucepan, bring to boil nonfat milk and nonfat milk powder, stirring continuously.
2. Reduce heat, add the remaining ingredients and simmer for 5 to 10 minutes, stirring continuously.
3. Serve hot.

Traditionally Kadho is served on festive occasions. It also makes a heart-warming drink, especially on cold days.

Nutrient Analysis (per serving):

Calories	154
Protein	10. 8 gm
Carbohydrates	22.1 gm
Total Fat	2.8 gm
Saturated Fat	0.6 gm
Cholesterol	5.2 mg
Sodium	150.0 mg

Rich Spiced Tea

For 4 servings you will need:

4   *cups nonfat milk*
1/4 *cup nonfat dry milk powder*
1/2 *cup water*
4   *whole cardamoms, slightly crushed*
1/4 *teaspoon ground ginger*
1/8 *teaspoon ground cloves*
1/8 *teaspoon ground cinnamon*
4   *teaspoons sugar (optional)*
1   *pinch saffron, crushed*
4   *tea bags*

To prepare:

1. In a heavy-bottomed saucepan, combine all ingredients except tea bags and bring to boil, stirring continuously.
2. Reduce heat and simmer for 5 minutes, stirring frequently.
3. Add tea bags and simmer for 2 minutes or until the tea is a rich almond color.
4. Remove from heat, strain and serve hot.

Indian Spiced Tea is served after a meal, with savory and sweet snacks, or on its own; a heart-warming drink, it is perfect for a cold day.

Nutrient Analysis (per serving):

Calories	120
Protein	9.9 gm
Carbohydrates	19.1 gm
Total Fat	0.5 gm
Saturated Fat	0.3 gm
Cholesterol	5.2 mg
Sodium	149.8 mg

Light Spiced Tea

For 4 servings you will need:

5   cups water
4   whole cardamoms, slightly crushed
1/4 teaspoon ground ginger
1/8 teaspoon ground cloves
1/8 teaspoon ground cinnamon
4   tea bags
1/2 cup nonfat milk (2 tablespoons per serving) *or* 8 teaspoons nonfat
    dry milk powder (2 teaspoons per serving)
4   teaspoons sugar (optional)

To prepare:

1.   In a saucepan, boil water, cardamoms, ginger, cloves and
     cinnamon for 5 minutes.
2.   Add tea bags, lower heat and simmer for 1 to 2 minutes.
3.   Remove from heat and strain into a warm teapot.
4.   Serve with nonfat milk or milk powder and sugar.

Nutrient Analysis (per serving):

Calories	30
Protein	1.1 gm
Carbohydrates	6.4 gm
Total Fat	0.1 gm
Saturated Fat	0 gm
Cholesterol	0.6 mg
Sodium	23.2 mg

Mint Yogurt Drink
Mint Lassi

For 4 servings you will need:

2   *cups nonfat yogurt*
2   *cups cold water*
1/4 *teaspoon ground black pepper*
1/2 *teaspoon cumin seeds, coarsely ground*
1/4 *cup fresh mint leaves, minced*
     crushed ice (optional)

To prepare:

1. Blend all the ingredients except ice in a blender until smooth. Chill until ready to serve.
2. Serve over crushed ice.

Variation: For Plain Lassi, omit mint leaves.

Nutrient Analysis (per serving):

Calories	65
Protein	6.6 gm
Carbohydrates	8.9 gm
Total Fat	0.3 gm
Saturated Fat	0.1 gm
Cholesterol	2.0 mg
Sodium	87.3 mg

Sweet Yogurt Drink
Mithi Lassi

For 4 servings you will need:

2   *cups nonfat yogurt*
1½ *cups cold water*
1/4 *teaspoon ground cardamom seeds*
4   *teaspoons sugar dissolved in 1/2 cup of hot water*
1/4 *teaspoon vanilla extract*
      crushed ice

To prepare:

1. Blend all the ingredients except ice in a blender until smooth.
2. Chill until ready to serve.
3. Serve over crushed ice.

Variation: Omit cardamoms and vanilla extract; instead add soft fruits such as strawberries, bananas, mangos, etc. in Step 1.

Nutrient Analysis (per serving):

Calories	81
Protein	6.5 gm
Carbohydrates	13.0 gm
Total Fat	0.2 gm
Saturated Fat	0.1 gm
Cholesterol	2.0 mg
Sodium	86.9 mg

Festive Milkshake
Sherbet

For 4 servings you will need:

1/2 *tablespoon takmaria (faludo seeds)*
4   *cups nonfat milk*
4   *teaspoons sugar dissolved in 1/4 cup hot water*
1/2 *teaspoon vanilla extract*
     enough red food color to produce a pleasant pink color
1   *tablespoon almonds, coarsely chopped*
1   *tablespoon pistachio, coarsely chopped*

To prepare:

1. Clean takmaria seeds and soak in water for 30 minutes or until seeds are well swollen.
2. In a jug, combine the remaining ingredients and stir well.
3. Strain takmaria, add to the Sherbet and stir.
4. Cover and chill until ready to serve.

Serve over crushed ice if preferred.

Nutrient Analysis (per serving):

Calories	122
Protein	9.1 gm
Carbohydrates	16.6 gm
Total Fat	2.2 gm
Saturated Fat	0.5 gm
Cholesterol	4.4 mg
Sodium	126.5 mg

Non-Indian Favorites

Coleslaw

For 6 servings you will need:

1   *medium tart cooking apple*
4   *tablespoons lemon juice*
2   *cups cabbage, shredded*
1   *cup carrots, peeled and shredded*
1/2 *green pepper, cut into 1-inch strips*
1   *small onion, finely diced*
1   *green chili, seeded and finely chopped (optional)*
1   *teaspoon garlic, minced*
1/4 *teaspoon salt (optional)*
1/4 *teaspoon red chili powder (optional)*
1/2 *teaspoon black mustard seeds, crushed*
1   *teaspoon sugar*
     freshly ground black pepper to taste

To prepare:

1.   Peel, core and shred the apple.
2.   In a bowl, combine shredded apple and lemon juice and mix well.
3.   Add the remaining ingredients, mix and chill until ready to serve.

Nutrient Analysis (per serving):

Calories	40
Protein	1.1 gm
Carbohydrates	9.8 gm
Total Fat	0.3 gm
Saturated Fat	0 gm
Cholesterol	0 mg
Sodium with salt included	102.8 mg
Sodium with salt omitted	13.1 mg

Potato Salad

For 4 servings you will need:

1   *pound potatoes*
1/4 *cup nonfat yogurt*
2   *tablespoons fat-free and cholesterol-free mayonnaise*
1   *tablespoon lemon juice*
1   *small onion, finely chopped*
1   *stalk celery, finely chopped*
1/2 *cup red sweet pepper, cut into 1-inch thin strips*
1   *green chili, seeded and finely chopped*
1/4 *cup cilantro, finely chopped*
1   *tablespoon parsley, finely chopped*
1/8 *teaspoon salt (optional)*
1/2 *teaspoon black mustard seeds, crushed*
     ground black pepper to taste
1   *tablespoon chives, chopped*
1/4 *teaspoon red chili powder* **or**
1/2 *teaspoon paprika*

To prepare:

1. In a saucepan, boil unpeeled potatoes until just cooked.
    When cool, peel and refrigerate for 30 minutes. Cut into
    1/2-inch cubes.
2. In a glass bowl, mix yogurt, mayonnaise and lemon juice.
3. Add potatoes and the remaining ingredients except chives
    and red chili powder or paprika and fold in.
4. Garnish with chives and red chili powder or paprika. Cover
    and chill until ready to serve.

Nutrient Analysis (per serving):

Calories	119
Protein	3.8 gm
Carbohydrates	26.2 gm
Total Fat	0.4 gm
Saturated Fat	0.1 gm
Cholesterol	0.3 mg
Sodium with salt included	189.8 mg
Sodium with salt omitted	122.6 mg

Guilt-free "French Fries"

For 4 servings you will need:

1   *pound potatoes*
    vegetable oil spray

To prepare:

1. Preheat oven to 450° F.
2. In a saucepan, boil unpeeled potatoes until just cooked;
    about 8 to 10 minutes. Drain, cool, peel and slice into strips.
3. Lightly spray a baking tray with vegetable oil spray. Arrange
    potato strips on the tray and lightly spray potatoes with oil.
4. Bake for 20 to 25 minutes or until the potatoes are crisp and
    golden. Serve immediately.

Nutrient Analysis (per serving):

Calories	92
Protein	2.4 gm
Carbohydrates	20.4 gm
Total Fat	0.4 gm
Saturated Fat	0.1 gm
Cholesterol	0 mg
Sodium	6.8 mg

Baked Potato

For 4 servings you will need:

4   *7-ounce potatoes*
1/2   *cup nonfat yogurt*
4   *teaspoons fresh chives, chopped*

To prepare:

1.   Scrub potatoes and prick with a fork. Place on a microwave-proof plate lined with paper towel.
2.   Cook in a microwave oven for 12 minutes at full power, turning over once half-way through cooking.
3.   Cut a deep cross on each potato and squeeze ends to open up. Garnish each potato with 2 tablespoons of nonfat yogurt and a teaspoon of chopped chives and serve.

Nutrient Analysis (per serving):

Calories	228
Protein	6.6 gm
Carbohydrates	51.0 gm
Total Fat	0.3 gm
Saturated Fat	0.1 gm
Cholesterol	0.5 mg
Sodium with salt omitted	37.8 mg

Vegetable Pizza

For 8 slices you will need:

For 1 cup Tomato Sauce

1/4   *cup celery, cut into small pieces*
1/4   *cup carrots, peeled and cut into pieces*
1   *tablespoon parsley, chopped*
2   *teaspoons olive oil*
1/2   *cup onions, quartered and finely sliced*
1   *large clove garlic, finely chopped*
1   *cup canned tomatoes without salt, blended*
4   *tablespoons tomato paste without salt*
1/4   *teaspoon dried basil*
1/2   *teaspoon dried oregano*
1/4   *teaspoon salt (optional)*
      freshly ground black pepper to taste

For the Topping

1   *zucchini, trimmed, halved and cut into 1/4" slices*
1   *cup small broccoli florets, sliced*
5   *small mushrooms, sliced*
1   *small onion, sliced*
1   *teaspoon olive oil*
4   *ounces low fat, low salt mozzarella cheese, grated (optional)*
1/2   *cup green pepper, cut into 1/2 inch square pieces*

For the Crust

1   *pizza crust (see page 234)*

To prepare:

1.   Preheat oven to 450° F.

To prepare sauce:

2.   In a blender blend celery, carrots and parsley to a near-smooth mixture.
3.   In a small saucepan, heat oil and sauté onions and garlic for 1 to 2 minutes, stirring frequently, until onions are soft.
4.   Add the blended mixture, mix and cook for 2 minutes, stirring frequently.
5.   Add the remaining sauce ingredients, mix and cook over low heat, until the sauce is thick and reduced to 1 cup.

Vegetable Pizza

To prepare topping:

6.   In a frying pan, heat 1 teaspoon oil and stir fry vegetables for 4 to 5 minutes. Remove from heat.

Finally

7.   Place the pizza crust on a pizza pan. Spread tomato sauce evenly over the crust. Arrange the cooked vegetables on top, sprinkle with cheese (if used) and garnish with green pepper.
8.   Bake in the preheated oven for 10 to 12 minutes or until the rim of the crust is golden and the cheese (if used) is bubbling.

Serve accompanied by tossed green salad.

Nutrient Analysis for Pizza with Cheese (per slice):

Calories	140
Protein	8.5 gm
Carbohydrates	20.8 gm
Total Fat	3.3 gm
Saturated Fat	1.3 gm
Cholesterol	4.0 mg
Sodium with salt included	188.7 mg
Sodium with salt omitted	88.0 mg

Nutrient Analysis for Pizza without cheese (per slice):

Calories	110
Protein	4.0 gm
Carbohydrates	20.3 gm
Total Fat	2.3 gm
Saturated Fat	0.3 gm
Cholesterol	0 mg
Sodium with salt included	118.7 mg
Sodium with salt omitted	17.9 mg

Tuna Salad Sandwich

For 5 servings you will need:

1/2 *cup onions, finely diced*
1/2 *cup celery, finely diced*
1/2 *cup green pepper, finely chopped*
1   *teaspoon canola oil*
1   *6½-ounce can Albacore tuna in water without salt, drained*
2   *tablespoons fat-free, cholesterol-free mayonnaise*
     freshly ground black pepper to taste
10   *slices whole-wheat bread*
10   *lettuce leaves*
2   *medium tomatoes, finely chopped*

To prepare:

1. In a microwave-proof dish combine and mix onions, celery, green pepper and oil. Microwave for 2 minutes.
2. Add drained tuna, flake with a fork and mix thoroughly well. Add mayonnaise and ground black pepper and mix well.
3. Make 5 sandwiches with bread slices layered with tuna mixture, lettuce and tomatoes.

Note: Use Pritikin bread instead of regular whole-wheat bread if you are on a low-sodium diet.

Nutrient Analysis (per serving):

Calories	207
Protein	15.5 gm
Carbohydrates	30.5 gm
Total Fat	3.6 gm
Saturated Fat	0.6 gm
Cholesterol	16.0 mg
Sodium	375.1 mg

Baked Salmon

For 8 servings you will need:

2   *pounds half salmon*
2   *tablespoons lemon juice*
1   *teaspoon canola oil*
2   *tablespoons water*

To prepare:

1. Preheat broiler, and oven to 400° F.
2. Clean and rinse fish and pat dry with paper towel.
3. Make 3 diagonal cuts on each side and pour lemon juice all over the fish.
4. Coat both sides of fish with oil and place on a foil-lined baking tray.
5. Broil for 4 minutes on each side.
6. Pour water by the side of the fish, wrap foil securely over the fish and bake in the preheated oven for 15 minutes.

Serve hot or cold with Baked Potatoes (page 211), Peas Pilav (page 100) and/or vegetables of your choice, accompanied by Cilantro Chutney (page 70) and lemon wedges.

Nutrient Analysis (per serving):

Calories	167
Protein	22.5 gm
Carbohydrates	0.3 gm
Total Fat	7.8 gm
Saturated Fat	1.2 gm
Cholesterol	62.4 mg
Sodium	49.9 mg

Turkey Burger

For 4 servings you will need:

1   *pound ground turkey breast meat*
1   *teaspoon garlic, minced*
1   *teaspoon root ginger, minced*
1   *green chili, seeded and minced (optional)*
1/2 *cup onions, finely chopped*
1   *teaspoon garam masala*
1/4 *teaspoon salt (optional)*
1   *tablespoon lemon juice*
4   *hamburger buns*
4   *lettuce leaves*
1   *medium tomato, sliced*
1   *medium onion, sliced into rounds*

To prepare:

1.   In a bowl, combine and mix turkey, garlic, ginger, green chili, onions, garam masala, salt and lemon juice.
2.   Form into 4 patties and broil or barbecue for 5 to 7 minutes on each side or until done.
3.   Serve on toasted buns layered with lettuce, tomato and onion slices.

Serve with Guilt-free "French Fries" (page 210)

Variation: Serve in Whole-wheat Naan pockets (page 176) with Salads, Pickles, Chutneys and Raita of you choice (page 61).

Nutrient Analysis (per serving):

Calories	391
Protein	35.0 gm
Carbohydrates	50.2 gm
Total Fat	3.8 gm
Saturated Fat	0.9 gm
Cholesterol	71.2 mg
Sodium with salt included	228.1 mg
Sodium with salt omitted	93.7 mg

Garlic Chicken

For 4 servings you will need:

4   *6-ounce chicken breasts*
1/4   *teaspoon salt (optional)*
1/4   *teaspoon dried parsley*
1   *teaspoon garlic powder*
     vegetable oil spray

To prepare:

1.   Preheat oven to 350° F.
2.   Remove skin and all visible fat from chicken breasts, rinse and pat dry.
3.   Place chicken breasts, meat side up, on a non-stick baking pan.
4.   Mix salt, parsley and garlic powder and sprinkle evenly over chicken breasts. Spray lightly with vegetable oil spray.
5.   Cover loosely with a piece of foil and bake for 40 minutes, removing the foil for the last 5 minutes.

Serve hot with Baked Potatoes (page 211) and vegetables of your choice.

Nutrient Analysis (per serving):

Calories	137
Protein	27.4 gm
Carbohydrates	0.5 gm
Total Fat	2.0 gm
Saturated Fat	0.4 gm
Cholesterol	68.4 mg
Sodium with salt included	210.2 mg
Sodium with salt omitted	75.6 mg

Omelette

For 1 servings you will need:

3   *egg whites*
2   *tablespoons onions, finely chopped*
1/2 *small tomato, finely diced*
1/2 *green chili, seeded and finely chopped*
1   *tablespoon cilantro, finely chopped*
1/2 *teaspoon canola oil*
1/16 *teaspoon salt (optional)*
    freshly ground black pepper to taste

To prepare:

1. In a bowl, beat egg whites. Add onions, tomatoes, green chilies, cilantro, salt and black pepper. Mix well.
2. Coat the base of an 8- to 9-inch (20 to 22 cm) nonstick shallow frying pan with 1/2 teaspoon oil.
3. Heat the pan and gently add the omelette mixture. Quickly tilt the pan in all directions so that the mixture covers the base. Lower the heat slightly and cook for 1 minute or until the underside is set.
4. With a spatula, fold in half and cook for further 1/2 minute. Gently turn over and cook for 1 minute.
5. Slide on a plate and serve.

Serve with Chapati (page 170), Paratha (pages 171, 172) or whole-wheat bread.

Nutrient Analysis (per serving):

Calories	99
Protein	11.8 gm
Carbohydrates	7.6 gm
Total Fat	2.6 gm
Saturated Fat	0.2 gm
Cholesterol	0 mg
Sodium with salt included	305.2 mg
Sodium with salt omitted	170.8 mg

Oat Bran Muffin

For 16 servings you will need:

4   *egg whites*
2   *tablespoons canola oil*
1/2 *cup sugar*
3/4 *cup nonfat milk*
2   *teaspoons vanilla extract*
2   *cups oat bran*
1/2 *cup all-purpose flour*
1   *tablespoon baking powder, low sodium*
1/4 *teaspoon salt (optional)*
1/4 *cup walnuts, chopped*
1/4 *cup raisins, seedless, tightly packed*
2   *teaspoons orange peel, grated*
     vegetable oil spray

To prepare:

1. Preheat oven to 350° F.
2. In a bowl, combine and beat egg whites, oil, sugar, nonfat milk and vanilla.
3. Add oat bran, all-purpose flour, baking powder, salt, nuts, raisins and orange peel, and beat with a wooden spoon for 2 to 3 minutes.
4. Spray two 7-inch (18 cm) cake pans lightly with vegetable oil spray. Pour the muffin mixture into the prepared cake pans and bake for 30 to 35 minutes until light brown. Test with a wooden toothpick. Muffins are ready when the toothpick comes out moist but clean.

If preferred bake in 16 individual muffin cups for about 20 to 25 minutes.

Nutrient Analysis (per serving):

Calories	113
Protein	4.0 gm
Carbohydrates	20.4 gm
Total Fat	3.9 gm
Saturated Fat	0.4 gm
Cholesterol	0.2 mg
Sodium with salt included	56.0 mg
Sodium with salt omitted	22.4 mg

Cheesecake

For 8 servings you will need:

3   *large egg whites*
3   *tablespoons sugar*
2   *cups lowfat (1%) cottage cheese*
1/2 *cup nonfat yogurt*
3   *tablespoons lemon juice*
3   *tablespoons all-purpose flour*
1   *teaspoon vanilla extract*

To prepare:

1. Preheat oven to 350° F.
2. In a food processor, combine and blend all the ingredients for 2 minutes or until smooth.
3. Pour into a 9-inch (22 cm) non-stick baking pan and bake in the preheated oven for 25 minutes or until firm.
4. When cool, refrigerate until ready to serve.

Serve on its own or with fresh fruit toppings of your choice, optionally with each serving accompanied by 1 Graham Cracker or Digestive Biscuit made with acceptable ingredients.

Nutrient Analysis (per serving):

Calories	86
Protein	9.5 gm
Carbohydrates	10.1 gm
Total Fat	0.6 gm
Saturated Fat	0.4 gm
Cholesterol	2.7 mg
Sodium	260.9 mg

Banana and Pear Sundae

For 4 servings you will need:

1   *16-ounce can pear halves in pear juice, with no sugar added*
2   *bananas*
1½ *cups ice milk (6 tablespoons per serving)*

To prepare:

1. Chill the can of pears in a refrigerator.
2. In a glass bowl, peel and cut bananas into round slices
3. Pour chilled pears and juice over sliced bananas and mix gently.
4. Serve in 4 individual bowls, topped with ice milk.

Nutrient Analysis (per serving):

Calories	178
Protein	2.9 gm
Carbohydrates	38.9 gm
Total Fat	2.5 gm
Saturated Fat	1.4 gm
Cholesterol	6.8 mg
Sodium with salt omitted	44.3 mg

Strawberry Milkshake

For 2 servings you will need:

1   *cup strawberries, hulled*
1   *small ripe banana, peeled and sliced*
1   *teaspoon sugar*
1   *cup cold nonfat milk*
1/2 *cup crushed ice*

To prepare:

1.   In a blender, process strawberries, banana and sugar until smooth.
2.   Add milk and blend for about 30 seconds until creamy.
3.   Add crushed ice and blend until frothy.
4.   Pour into 2 glasses and serve immediately

Nutrient Analysis (per serving):

Calories	122
Protein	4.9 gm
Carbohydrates	26.1 gm
Total Fat	0.8 gm
Saturated Fat	0.3 gm
Cholesterol	2.0 mg
Sodium	59.7 mg

Basic Recipes and Methods

Nonfat Cheese
Paneer

You will need:

8   *cups nonfat milk*
4   *tablespoons lemon juice*

To prepare:

1. Stand a large strainer lined with cheese cloth in a large bowl.
2. In a large heavy-bottomed saucepan, slowly bring milk to boil. Add lemon juice and stir until the milk curdles, lumps form and clear whey separates. Remove from heat and allow to stand for a few minutes
3. Strain in the prepared strainer, and allow whey to drain.
4. Shape the cheese while still in the cloth into a ball and flatten slightly.   Fold the cloth over the cheese and place on a flat surface. Place a weight (a saucepan filled with water will do) on the cheese for 20 minutes to squeeze out any remaining whey.

This will yield a flat round of Paneer about 1/4-inch thick.

Cubed Paneer is cooked with vegetable curries (pages 90, 92); whey can be used for making curries, sauces, soups and gravies.

Nutrient Analysis (per recipe):

Calories	700
Protein	67.1 gm
Carbohydrates	100.3 gm
Total Fat	3.5 gm
Saturated Fat	2.3 gm
Cholesterol	35.3 mg
Sodium	1010.0 mg

Nonfat Yogurt

For 4 cups you will need:

4   *cups nonfat milk*
1/4   *cup nonfat plain yogurt**

To prepare:

1.   In a heavy saucepan, bring milk to boil.
2.   Pour milk into a Pyrex bowl and allow to cool to 110° F (or just hot enough to hold your little finger in it without burning).
3.   Add yogurt and stir thoroughly.
4.   Cover with plastic wrap and a clean towel and keep in a warm draught-free place where it does not get disturbed (an oven with a pilot light is ideal) for 3 to 4 hours or until yogurt sets.
5.   Refrigerate until ready to use.

* Note: Store-bought yogurt will do as a starter; yogurt made with milk, without added ingredients such gelatine is best.

Nutrient Analysis (per cup):

Calories	93
Protein	9.2 gm
Carbohydrates	13.0 gm
Total Fat	0.5 gm
Saturated Fat	0.1 gm
Cholesterol	4.7 mg
Sodium	137.0 mg

Nonfat 'Sour Cream'

For 2 cups you will need:

32   ounces (4 cups) nonfat yogurt

To prepare:

1. Stand a large strainer lined with cheese cloth in a bowl large enough to hold at least 2 cups of whey.
2. Pour yogurt in the lined strainer and let it drain for at least 20 minutes.
3. Skim off the drained yogurt in a glass bowl and mix well. Refrigerate until ready to use.

Whenever a recipe calls for sour cream, use this 'nonfat' sour cream instead.

Nutrient Analysis (per cup):

Calories	253
Protein	26.0 gm
Carbohydrates	34.8 gm
Total Fat	0.8 gm
Saturated Fat	0.5 gm
Cholesterol	8.2 mg
Sodium	347.0 mg

Tamarind Sauce

For 4 cups you will need:

4½ cups water
1/2 pound tamarind

To prepare:

1. In a saucepan, bring 4 cups water to boil. Add tamarind, cook for 10 minutes, and allow to cool.
2. Press with the back of a spoon or fingers to soften tamarind. Squeeze to extract juice and pulp.
3. Strain into a glass bowl, forcing as much pulp as possible through the strainer and scraping pulp from the underside of the strainer into the bowl.
4. Return the residue left in the strainer to the saucepan and add 1/2 cup of warm water. Press with spoon to extract remaining juice and pulp.
5. Repeat step 3. Discard residue.
6. Cover and refrigerate until ready to use.

This sauce is used for making Chutneys (pages 71, 72). It can also be used in vegetarian dishes instead of lemon juice. It makes an ideal salt -and sugar-free dip or salad dressing.

Nutrient Analysis (per cup):

Calories	68
Protein	0.8 gm
Carbohydrates	17.7 gm
Total Fat	0.2 gm
Saturated Fat	0.1 gm
Cholesterol	0 mg
Sodium	7.9 mg

Garam Masala

To make 2½ ounces you will need:

Traditional Method

1½ ounces cinnamon sticks, broken into small pieces
1/2 ounce cardamom seeds, extracted from the pods
1/2 ounce whole cloves

To prepare:

1. Combine all the ingredients and grind into a fine powder in a coffee grinder.
2. Store in an airtight container and use as required.

Garam Masala ingredients may be lightly roasted for 1 to 2 minutes on a griddle, or for 8 to 10 minutes in an oven preheated to 150° F, before grinding.

Quick and Easy Method

1½ ounces ground cinnamon
1/2 ounce groundcardamom
1/2 ounce ground cloves

To prepare:

1. Combine all the ingredients and mix well
2. Store in an airtight container and use as required.

Garam Masala is used in many Indian dishes to give zest and aroma.

Nutrient Analysis (per recipe):

Calories	201
Protein	4.0 gm
Carbohydrates	52.3 gm
Total Fat	5.2 gm
Saturated Fat	1.0 gm
Cholesterol	0 mg
Sodium	48.2 mg

Sprouted Mung

For 2 cups you will need:

1   *cup whole mung beans*
6   *cups water*

To prepare:

1.   Clean and wash mung thoroughly and soak in water for at least 12 hours.
2.   Drain and wash several times in water.
3.   Put the drained mung in a piece of clean, damp cloth, tie it loosely and place in a bowl.
4.   Place the bowl in a warm, dark place for 2 to 3 days. Keep the cloth damp by sprinkling water over it 2 to 3 times a day.
5.   Check every morning to see if mung beans have sprouted; continue until the sprouts are about 1/2 to 3/4 inch long.

Sprouted Mung can be cooked into delicious salads and curries (page 66). Sprouted Mung can also be used uncooked in salads.

Nutrient Analysis (per recipe):

Calories	62
Protein	6.3 gm
Carbohydrates	12.3 gm
Total Fat	0.4 gm
Saturated Fat	0.1 gm
Cholesterol	0 mg
Sodium	12.5 mg

Samosa Pastry

For 24 strips you will need:

2   *cups all-purpose flour*
     water
3½ *teaspoons canola oil*
     all-purpose flour for dusting

To Prepare:

1.   In a large bowl sift flour. Make a well in the center, add water slowly and make a pliable dough (see page 235). Knead well.
2.   Divide dough into 8 equal portions. Roll out each portion on a floured flat surface into a 6-inch (15 cm) round, dusting lightly with flour as necessary.
3.   Brush the top of a round evenly with 1/2 teaspoon of oil and dust with flour. Carefully place another round on top, brush with oil and dust with flour. Continue the process using up all the rounds. Do not brush the top of the last round with oil.
4.   Carefully roll out the stack of rounds, turning over and dusting as necessary, until 11½ inches (28 cm) in diameter.
5.   Lift the round with a rolling pin and place it on a preheated griddle. Lower the heat immediately and cook for 30 seconds. Turn it over and carefully peel off the top layer (pastry) and place on a plate. Turn over the round again and peel off the top layer and stack on the plate. Repeat this process until all the rounds are done.
6.   Cut the stack of cooked pastry rounds into three equal strips as illustrated in Figures 1 and 2, making 24 strips in all. Keep strips covered in a damp cloth or in a plastic ziplock bag until ready to use.

Author's tip: Do not throw away the off-cuts which result from cutting the pastry into strips. These make the tastiest flour chips. Spread off-cuts on a nonstick baking tray. Spray lightly with vegetable oil spray and bake in a 400° F preheated oven for 5 minutes or until crisp and light golden. Serve immediately, or cool and store in an airtight container until needed.

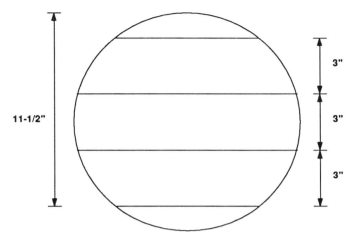

Figure 1. Cutting strips from pastry

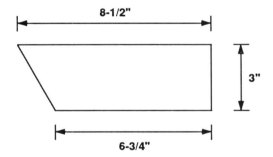

Figure 2. Cut strips from Fig. 1 into this shape

(You may find it easier if you use a paper template of the above shape)

Nutrient Analysis (per strip as in Fig 2):

Calories	31
Protein	0.8 gm
Carbohydrates	5.6 gm
Total Fat	0.6 gm
Saturated Fat	0.1 gm
Cholesterol	0 mg
Sodium	0.2 mg

Folding and Filling Samosa

For 24 Samosa you will need:

3 *tablespoons all-purpose flour*
2 *tablespoons water*
1 *recipe Vegetable, Turkey, Chicken or Beef Samosa*
       (pages 42, 48, 52, 56), includes
       24 Samosa Pastry Strips and Samosa Filling

To prepare:

1. In a small bowl, make a smooth paste by mixing flour and
    water .
2. Fold a pastry strip into an envelope, as illustrated in Figures 3
    and 4.
3. Hold the envelope firmly as shown in Figure 5 and fill with
    the filling.
4. Smear the flap of the envelope with the paste, fold over and
    seal the envelope. The Samosa should now look as in
    Figure 6.
5. Repeat steps 2, 3 and 4 for each strip.
6. Place Samosa on a plate, cover and refrigerate until ready to
    fry.

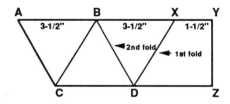

Figure 3. Lines BC, BD and DX are fold lines

1. Fold along line XD so that the edge DZ lines up with the fold
    line BD
2. Fold along line BD; the envelop should now look as
    illustrated in Figure 4

Folding and Filling Samosa

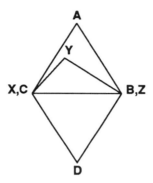

Figure 4. Envelope after 1st and 2nd folds

Figure 5. Holding Samosa envelope for filling

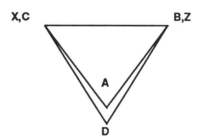

Figure 6. Samosa after filling and sealing the flap

Pizza Crust

For 2 pizza crusts you will need:

1   *teaspoon sugar*
3/4 *cup warm water, about 110° F*
1/4 *ounce envelope rapid-rise dry yeast*
1½   *cups whole wheat flour*
3/4 *cup all-purpose flour*
1/4 *teaspoon salt (optional)*
     vegetable oil spray

To prepare:

1. In a jug, combine sugar and warm water. Add yeast, stir and let stand for 5 minutes until frothy on the top.
2. In a large bowl, mix both the flours and salt . Make a well in the center, pour in the yeast mixture and make dough.
3. Knead the dough on a lightly floured surface for 6 to 7 minutes until smooth. (See page 235).
4. Shape dough into a ball and return to the bowl. Cover the bowl with plastic wrap and a clean towel. Keep in a warm place for 30 minutes to rise.
5. Preheat oven to 450° F.
6. Spray two 11-inch (28 cm) round baking trays with vegetable oil spray.
7. Punch and knead dough and divide into 2 equal portions and roll each portion into an 11-inch (28 cm) round.
8. Place pizza rounds on the prepared baking trays, prick with a fork and bake in the preheated oven for 5 to 6 minutes.
9. Remove and allow to cool. Refrigerate until ready to use.

For Vegetable Pizza filling see page 212.

Nutrient Analysis (per crust):

Calories	493
Protein	18.5 gm
Carbohydrates	104.4 gm
Total Fat	2.2 gm
Saturated Fat	0.4 gm
Cholesterol	0 mg
Sodium with salt included	273.7 mg
Sodium with salt omitted	5.0 mg

Making Dough for Breads

For successful bread-making, it is important to get the dough right. In this book you will find recipes for unleavened bread (Chapati, Paratha, Poori, Rotlo and Samosa Pastry), and for leavened bread (Naan and Pizza Crust). The following tips will help you prepare dough for the various breads.

In all the bread recipes in this book the amount of water is approximate. The exact amount you will need depends on the flour (which varies from batch to batch) and the humidity in the air. Therefore, add water gradually and bind and knead to produce a smooth and moldable (pliable and elastic) dough. This will make it easy to roll and cook the breads.

If you use too little water, the dough will be hard and will split and crack at the edges when you roll. In this case, sprinkle some water over the dough, a little at a time, and knead until you obtain the right consistency.

If you use too much water, the dough will feel sticky and will be difficult to roll. In this case, sprinkle some flour over the dough, a little at a time, and knead until the dough is just right. With a little practice making good dough will become second nature.

The foregoing applies to all breads except Rotlo, which is made with millet flour and does not produce an elastic dough. However, add enough water to make a moldable dough. Traditionally, the dough is shaped into a flat round Rotlo entirely by hand and slapped onto a preheated griddle. This process requires practice to perfect. In this book, a slightly elaborate, but easier and more workable procedure is described.

Preparing Peas, Beans, Lentils and Rice for Cooking

Peas and Beans

Preparation for cooking peas and beans (such as black-eyed peas, chick-peas, mung beans, etc.) involves sorting, washing and soaking. Store-bought peas and beans are likely to contain tiny pebbles or hard shrivelled-up peas or beans; these should be picked out. After sorting, peas and beans should be washed to remove any dust and then soaked in cold water for at least 4 to 5 hours, or overnight. After soaking, wash in cold water several times and drain before cooking. This process has two benefits: first, it gets rid of all the dust, and second, it removes some of the sugars that upset the digestive system of individuals who are sensitive to peas and beans. (In Indian cooking it is believed that the use of root ginger in cooking alleviates the digestive discomfort resulting from eating beans.)

The first few minutes of boiling peas and beans produces froth in the cooking vessel. It is best to skim this off.

Lentils

Lentils are split (and oftentimes hulled) peas and beans. These, too, should be sorted to remove foreign objects. After sorting, the lentils should be washed in cold water several times to remove dust. Toor or Toovar lentils are sometimes sold coated with oil to increase shelf life; these lentils should be washed in warm water. Unless specified in a recipe, it is not generally necessary to soak lentils before cooking.

Rice

Most of the rice recipes in this book call for Basmati rice. This rice comes from India and Pakistan. If Basmati rice is unavailable use long grain rice. Before cooking, rice should be washed in several changes of water.

For Your Information

About Indian Ingredients and Spices

Most of the ingredients used in this book are readily available from regular food stores. Ingredients which are typically Indian can be obtained from Indian grocery stores, of which there are many in most cities of the world. Below is a glossary of ingredients used in recipes in this book whose common names are listed in alphabetical order with their Indian translations, where appropriate, in parenthesis:

Agar-agar (Chinese Grass or Chinese Gelatine): is a vegetable gelatine derived from certain kinds of seaweed. It is used as a setting agent.

Almonds (Badam): are used blanched or unblanched, for making and garnishing sweets and desserts.

Asafetida (Hing): is a strong-smelling resin, reputed to prevent flatulence. It is used sparingly to flavor some vegetable dishes.

Basmati Rice: is an aromatic long-grain rice from India and Pakistan. It is considered to be the King of rice. If Basmati rice is not available, other long-grain rice may be used.

Black Pepper (Mari): is used both whole and in powdered form as a spice.

Bulgar (Lapsi): is coarsely crushed wheat which comes in various grades of coarseness. It is called Lapsi in Indian stores and Bulgar in Mid-East stores.

Butter Oil: See Ghee

Cardamoms (Elaichi)*: are green, white, or black pods which contain black seeds. Cardamoms are very aromatic when crushed. Some recipes require whole cardamoms, while others require crushed seeds only. Recipes in this book only use green or white cardamoms.

Chana Daal: are split and hulled chickpeas. See Daal

Chickpea Flour (Besan): is flour made out of chickpeas. It is also known as Gram flour.

Chickpeas (Chana): come is two varieties, light (Garbanzo or Kabuli chana) and dark brown (kala chana).

Chili Powder, Red (Lal Mirchi): is ground hot red chilies. If unavailable, Cayenne Pepper may be used instead.

Chilies, Green (Mirchi): are hot green chilies; Jalapeno or Serano chilies are ideal, but if you do not like the hot taste, a milder variety can be used for flavor.

Cilantro (Lila Dhania or Kothmir): are fresh green coriander leaves used extensively in savory dishes and for garnishing.

Cinnamon (Taj)*: is the inner bark of cinnamon trees which has a sweetish taste and a pleasant flavor. It is used both in 'stick' and powdered forms.

Citric Acid (Limboo na Phool): is used instead of lemon juice.

Cloves (Laving)*: have a wonderful aroma and are used whole or in powdered form as a spice.

Coriander (Dhania)*: are seeds of the coriander or cilantro plant. They are generally used in coarsely or finely ground powdered forms as a spice. Also see Cilantro.

Cream of Wheat (Sooji): is also known as Semolina and is used for making both savory and sweet dishes.

Cumin (Jeera)*: is a wonderfully aromatic seed. It is used whole or in powdered form as a spice.

Curry Leaves (Limbdo): are aromatic leaves which can be bought fresh or dried, and used in curries.

Daal: is a variety of hulled or unhulled split lentils. Daals used in recipes in this book are Chana (split Chickpeas), Masoor (split salmon colored Red Lentil), Mung (split Mung Beans), Toor or Toovar (pale yellow daal from split pigeon peas) and Urad (split Black Mung). A dish made out of lentils is also called Daal. Lentils are very rich in protein and make a good substitute for meat. Before cooking, daals should be sorted, washed and rinsed in water (see page 236).

Eno's Fruit Salt: is an English product readily available in Indian grocery stores and is used as a raising agent. You can make its equivalent by combining 1 ounce baking soda, 1/2 ounce tartaric acid and 1/3 ounce citric acid: store in an airtight container and use as required.

Fennel Seeds (Variari or Sauf): are aromatic seeds which taste similar to anise seed and are used whole in cooking. Roasted seeds make a delicious mouth freshener.

Fenugreek Seeds (Methi): are tiny yellow cube-shaped seeds used whole or crushed for cooking and making pickles.

Garam Masala*: is a very aromatic spice mixture made out of cinnamon, cloves and cardamoms. See recipe on page 228.

Garlic (Lasan): Once shunned in the West, it now needs no explanation. Mostly used minced, cloves can be peeled and minced in small quantities and stored in a refrigerator a few days at a time. Spring garlic is also used in certain dishes.

Ghee: is clarified butter, also known as Butter Oil. It has a high content of both saturated fatty acid and cholesterol. It is not recommended for a heart-healthy diet.

Ginger, Root (Adu or Adrak): is fresh root ginger, mostly used in minced form. Peel before using. Small quantities of minced ginger can be stored in a refrigerator for a few days at a time.

Ginger, Ground (Soonth): is powdered dried root ginger.

Jaggery (Ghoor): is sold as hard or semi-soft pieces of unrefined cane sugar. It varies in color from light golden brown to very dark brown, has a unique flavor close to that of molasses, and is used in many Indian recipes instead of sugar.

Lentils, split (Daal): See Daal

Lentils, whole: Lentils are prevalent in Indian cooking. Rich in protein, a variety of whole lentils are used in recipes in this book. These are: dark brown chickpeas (kala chana), light chickpeas (Garbanzo or Kabuli); Mung Beans (olive green); Masoor (dark brown); and Urad (black). Also see Daal. (See page 236 for preparation tips).

Masoor Daal: are hulled and split salmon colored Red Lentils. See Daal

Mung Daal: are hulled or unhulled and split Mung beans. See Daal

Mustard Seeds, Whole Black (Rai): are black round seeds with a stronger taste and flavor than their yellow counterpart. These are available and used both whole and coarsely ground.

Nutmeg (Jaiphal): is a deliciously aromatic nut and is best used freshly crushed or grated. In powdered form it loses flavor rapidly.

Omum (Ajma): are small aromatic seeds used in some vegetarian dishes.

Pistachio nuts (Pista): are used for making and garnishing sweets and desserts.

Saffron (Kesar): are aromatic orange-colored stigmas of a crocus flower sometimes known as vegetable gold. It is the most expensive spice of all, and is used for flavoring festive dishes. Although also available in powdered form, it is best used in the form of stigmas. Buy in small quantities and store in an airtight container.

Semolina (Sooji): See Cream of Wheat

Sesame Seeds (Til): are beige seeds used in cooking; or roasted, slightly salted and served as a mouth freshener.

Takmaria (Faludo Seeds): are tiny black seeds which swell when soaked in water. They are added to Sherbet (Indian milk-shake).

Tamarind (Ambli or Imli): is a bean-like fruit. When ripe the pod covering is peeled off and the fruit is seeded. It is available packaged as compressed slabs. Concentrated tamarind pulp is also available. The fruit has a wonderful sweet-and-sour taste and is used for making a variety of chutneys or dips and is also used in cooking.

Toor or Toovar Daal: are pale yellow split pigeon peas, sometimes sold coated with oil to increase shelf life; this daal should be washed in warm water before using. See Daal.

Turmeric (Haldi)*: is a rhizome of the ginger family. It is bright yellow and is used in powdered form as a spice to add color and flavor to savory dishes. It is reputed to have remarkable medicinal properties.

Urad Daal: Hulled and split Black Mung Daal. Also see Daal

Vermicelli (Sev): a thin spaghetti type pasta which can be bought both in straight and coiled forms. Use only the egg-free variety.

Yellow Food Color: is used for coloring both savory and sweet dishes. It is available in powdered form from Indian stores; the powdered form should be dissolved in a little water before using. If unavailable, liquid yellow food coloring can be used.

* Spices lose flavor rapidly after being ground. For best results, buy freshly ground spices from stores, or grind whole spices in small quantities and store in airtight containers.

Whole spices such as whole cardamoms, black peppercorns, cloves, and cinnamon sticks are used in cooking for flavoring dishes. These should be discarded when eating the food.

Conversion Tables for Weights, Measures and Energy

Quantities given in this book are in standard American measures. Outside the United States most countries use metric measures or British Imperial measures. Tables in this chapter are provided to facilitate preparation of dishes from recipes in this book.

WEIGHTS

American	British	Metric
Ounces/Pounds	Ounces/Pounds	Grams (to nearest 5)
1 oz	1 oz	30 gms
2 oz	2 oz	55 gms
3 oz	3 oz	85 gms
4 oz	4 oz	115 gms
5 oz	5 oz	140 gms
6 oz	6 oz	170 gms
7 oz	7 oz	200 gms
8 oz	8 oz	225 gms
9 oz	9 oz	255 gms
10 oz	10 oz	285 gms
11 oz	11 oz	310 gms
12 oz	12 oz	340 gms
13 oz	13 oz	370 gms
14 oz	14 oz	395 gms
15 oz	15 oz	425 gms
16 oz	16 oz	455 gms
1/4 pound	1/4 pound	115 gms
1/2 pound	1/2 pound	225 gms
3/4 pound	3/4 pound	340 gms
1 pound	1 pound	455 gms

VOLUMETRIC MEASURES

Although many American, British, Canadian and Australian measures have identical names, the measures are not the same. The tables in this section provide the conversion information.

American	American	British	Metric
Measure	Volume		(approx.)
1/4 cup	2 fl oz	2 fl oz	55 ml
1/2 cup	4 fl oz	4 fl oz	110 ml
3/4 cup	6 fl oz	6 fl oz	170 ml
1 cup	8 fl oz	8 fl oz	225 ml
2 cups	16 fl oz	16 fl oz	450 ml
1/4 tsp	1/24 fl oz	1/4 tsp	1.25 ml
1/2 tsp	1/12 fl oz	1/2 tsp	2.5 ml
3/4 tsp	1/8 fl oz	3/4 tsp	3.75 ml
1 tsp	1/6 fl oz	1 tsp	5 ml
1 tbsp	1/2 fl oz or 3 tsp	8/10 tbsp or 3 tsp	15 ml

Notes for British Readers

The British 1/2 pint cup holds 10 fluid ounces, whereas the American cup holds 8 fluid ounces: therefore use an 8 fluid ounce measure whenever a recipe calls for 1 cup. The teaspoon in both countries is equal, but the British tablespoon is about 1¼ times larger than the American tablespoon -- therefore use 3 teaspoons or just over 3/4 British tablespoon for each American tablespoon.

Notes for Australian Readers

The standard measuring cup in Australia is 250 ml, the teaspoon is the same measure as the American teaspoon (5 ml), but the tablespoon is larger (20 ml), equal to 4 teaspoons. Therefore, use 3/4 Australian tablespoon measure wherever the recipes in this book call for 1 tablespoon.

LINEAR MEASURES

Imperial	Metric (approx.)
1 inch	2.5 cm
3 inches	7.5 cm
6 inches	15.5 cm
9 inches	22.5 cm
12 inches (1 foot)	30.5 cm

ENERGY

Energy content of recipes in this book is given in calories, the unit of energy measure generally used in the U.S.A. Many countries use the joule as the unit of energy. The conversion factor is:

1 calorie = 4.184 kilojoules (4.2 kjoules approximately)

OVEN TEMPERATURES

Degrees F	Degrees C	Gas Mark
250° F	120° C	1/2
275° F	135° C	1
300° F	150° C	2
325° F	160° C	3
350° F	175° C	4
375° F	190° C	5
400o F	205° C	6
425° F	220° C	7
450° F	230° C	8
475° F	250° C	9

Understanding Fats and Oils

All fats and oils contain three types of fatty acids: saturated, polyunsaturated and monounsaturated. In addition, fats from animal sources also contain cholesterol. A table of fats and oils with the analysis of these four components is given on page 248.

Saturated Fatty Acids

Fats and oils high in saturated fatty acids tend to solidify and become hard at room temperature. Butter, lard, beef fat, and tropical oils such as coconut, palm and palm kernel are examples of such fats.

Saturated fat in diet raises blood cholesterol level, and therefore oils and fats used for cooking and eating should be those with least amount of saturated fat.

Polyunsaturated and Monounsaturated Fats

Oils high in unsaturated fats, that is, those with high content of polyunsaturated and monounsaturated fats stay liquid at room temperature.

Polyunsaturated Fatty Acids

The polyunsaturated fat content of oils tends to help lower blood cholesterol; however, it is thought to reduce both bad cholesterol (LDL) and good cholesterol (HDL). Corn, safflower, soybean and sunflower are examples of oils which have a high content of polyunsaturated fatty acids.

Monounsaturated Fatty Acids

Recent studies seem to indicate that monounsaturated fats tend to lower the levels of bad cholesterol (LDL) only, without affecting the level of good cholesterol (HDL), although earlier it was thought that monunsaturated fats had no effect on cholesterol at all. In light of the new indications, oils with a higher level of monounsaturated fatty acids are recommended. Examples of such oils are canola (rapeseed) oil, olive oil, and peanut oil.

Hydrogenated and Partially-hydrogenated Oils

Oils which are ordinarily liquid at room temperature are often artificially hardened to make margarines and shortenings for cooking and baking. Hydrogenation raises the saturated fat content and thus hydrogenated oils tend to raise the level of blood cholesterol. Many stores sell oils such as canola and corn which have been hydrogenated and are solid at room temperatures. These oils are not recommended.

Margarines

Margarines are produced by partially saturating oils in order to harden them at room temperature. Therefore, although margarines are better than butter, they are not as good as liquid oil. Tub margarines are considered to be better than stick margarines. Always look for margarines which are made out of one of the acceptable oils, such as canola or corn, and that have liquid oil listed as the first ingredient and hydrogenated oil as the second.

Dietary Goals

Too much fat in your diet is bad for you. Apart from its high caloric content which can lead to obesity, too much fat in diet is reputed to increase the risk of certain types of cancers and can lead to other physical disorders. Total fat calories in your diet should be less than 30% of total calories according to the American Heart Association, and of which, saturated fat calories should be less than 10%; the lesser the better. (Please note: 1 gram of fat equals about 9 calories).

In practice, this means that if you are on an 1800 calories per day diet, you should not consume more than 540 fat calories or 60 grams of fat per day from all sources. You are likely to get half of this fat from food ingredients and prepared foods. So the rule of thumb is that you should use no more than 6 to 7 teaspoons of oil and/or margarine per day for cooking and eating at the table. For a family, set aside two tablespoons (6 teaspoons) of fat (oil and margarine) per person per day. This will ensure that you will not exceed the recommended limit of fat calories.

The Nutrient Analysis for every recipe in this book provides information on the recipe's Total Fat and Saturated Fat content. Please also read "About Recipes in this Book" (see page 12).

Comparison of Dietary Fats and Oils

FAT	CHOLESTEROL mg/tbsp	SATURATED FAT %	POLY- UNSATURATED FAT %	MONO- UNSATURATED FAT %
Canola Oil	0	6	32	62
Safflower Oil	0	10	77	13
Sunflower Oil	0	11	69	20
Corn Oil	0	13	62	25
Olive Oil	0	14	9	77
Soybean Oil	0	15	61	24
Peanut Oil	0	18	33	49
Margarine	0	19	32	49
Cottonseed Oil	0	27	54	19
Vegetable Shortening	0	28	28	44
Palm Oil	0	53	10	37
Palm Kernel Oil	0	86	2	12
Coconut Oil	0	91	2	7
Chicken Fat	11	31	22	47
Lard	12	41	12	47
Lamb Fat	13	51	8	41
Beef Fat	14	52	4	44
Butter (Ghee)	36	66	4	30

Comparison of vegetable and animal dietary fats listed in order of increasing saturated fat content.

Please note that the least amount of saturated fat is best.

Understanding Proteins

Protein is one of the most important nutrients for the body. It is essential for growth, maintenance and repair of cells from which our internal organs, muscle tissues, bones, skin and hair are made. Its vital functions include: production of red cells in the blood which carry oxygen to all body tissues; production of enzymes and hormones that control chemical processes and bodily functions; and production of antibodies to fight infections.

If the body does not get enough carbohydrates or fat to meet its energy needs, it converts proteins into energy. If the body gets excess protein, it stores it as fat, since it has no way of storing it in its original form.

The body's protein requirements can be met by eating a wide variety of foods from animal and/or vegetable sources. A balanced diet derived from the four basic food groups will ensure adequate protein intake. Foods rich in protein are fish, poultry, meat, low- or non-fat milk products and legumes (peas, beans, lentils).

Dietary Goals

The amount of protein required by the body depends on body size. Pregnant and lactating women and babies need a little extra. For persons older than 15 years, the Recommended Dietary Allowances published by the National Research Council in the U.S.A. suggest 0.8 grams of protein per kilogram (2.2 pounds) weight. This means that a person weighing about 135 pounds will need 50 grams of protein per day.

It is very easy to satisfy the protein needs of the body. For example a cup or an 8-ounce glass of nonfat milk contains 9 grams of protein; a 3-ounce piece of cooked chicken breast meat contains about 27 grams of protein; a cup of cooked lentils contains about 18 grams; a one-ounce slice of whole wheat bread contains 4 grams.

The Nutrient Analysis for each recipe in this book provides information on the recipe's protein content. Please also read "About Recipes in this Book" (see page 12).

Understanding Carbohydrates

To many people carbohydrates mean foods like rice, bread, potatoes and pasta. However, carbohydrates are present in many foods, such as fruits, vegetables and dairy products. The two main types of carbohydrates are starches and sugars. All carbohydrates are eventually turned by the body into glucose to provide the energy it needs.

Sugars in diet are known as simple carbohydrates. These simple sugars, such as those found in cane sugar and candies, are known as empty calories since they lack other nutrients and provide only energy. Starches are complex carbohydrates which are found in nearly all plant foods such as grains, legumes, vegetables and fruits. These foods tend to be high in nutrients because they contain protein, vitamins, minerals, and fiber, in addition to energy. Complex carbohydrates also help to maintain a more stable blood sugar level because of their slower rate of metabolism by the body. A healthful diet should contain a good share of complex carbohydrates.

Fiber, a form of complex carbohydrate, comes in two types: insoluble and soluble. The insoluble form is reputed to provide protection against cancer of the colon. Soluble fiber is nutritious and is believed to lower blood cholesterol. Foods rich in complex carbohydrates are also valuable sources of fiber.

Dietary Goals

Contrary to general belief, carbohydrates are not fattening. One gram of carbohydrates provides only 4 calories compared to fat which provides 9 calories per gram. So you can eat more than twice the amount of carbohydrates instead of fat. Moreover complex carbohydrates are more sustaining and nutritious than fat. For a healthful diet, it is recommended that 50% to 60% of daily calories should be derived from carbohydrates, and most preferably from the complex variety.

The Nutrient Analysis for each recipe in this book provides information on the recipe's carbohydrate content.

Understanding Sodium and Salt

Whereas sodium is an essential nutrient in diet, it is also associated with high blood pressure or hypertension, a very dangerous disease. For some people, too much sodium raises blood pressure beyond safe limits. Since hypertension is one of several symptomless diseases, and many people do not even know that they have it, it is recommended that sodium in a diet should be limited to less than 3,000 milligrams for all healthy adults. Individuals who have hypertension are advised to reduce their sodium intake to a minimum. The actual daily amount needed by the body is just a few hundred milligrams for most people.

All foods contain some natural sodium. For example, a cup of nonfat milk contains about 126 milligrams of sodium, and one stalk of celery contains about 35 milligrams. In most balanced diets, all the body's sodium needs are provided naturally.

Nearly all the excess sodium in a diet comes from salt and other sodium containing ingredients used in cooking and added to the food at the table. One teaspoon of salt contains nearly 2150 milligrams of sodium. Processed and fast foods are notoriously high in sodium content; for example, just one McDonald's Big Mac contains over 950 milligrams, and the Fillet-O-Fish contains over 1000 milligrams (about one-third your total daily allowance). Prepared foods such as most varieties of pickles, canned soups, dry cereals and grocery store breads also tend to be very high in salt and sodium content.

Dietary Goals

For a healthful diet, sodium should be limited to less than 3,000 milligrams per day (from all sources) for a healthy adult. Individuals with high blood pressure should be guided by their physicians.

The Nutrient Analysis for each recipe in this book provides information on the recipe's sodium content with and without added salt. Salt is always listed as optional. Please also read "About Recipes in this Book" (see page 12).

Understanding Calories

One of the major functions of food that we eat is to provide nutrients for bodily growth, maintenance, repair and vital functions. Food's other major function is to act as fuel to provide energy. This energy is measured in units called calories. Energy is also measured in joules; 1 calorie equals approximately 4.2 kilojoules.

Calorie content of different foods vary; for example, fats yield about 9 calories per gram, carbohydrates and proteins yield about 4 calories per gram, and water and insoluble fiber have no calories. Thus, foods such as most fruits and vegetables which have a high content of water and fiber are low in calories. On the other hand, fried foods and nuts which have a high fat content, are high in calories.

When a body gets more calories than it needs through diet, whether in the form of fats, proteins or carbohydrates, the excess calories are stored as fat in the body and result in weight gain. Conversely, if a person consumes fewer calories than needed, the body will convert the stored fat into energy, resulting in weight loss.

How many calories do you need per day?

A body's energy needs depend on many factors, such as age, growth rate, sex, body weight, body composition, climate, and physical activity.

Given all these factors, one can only estimate the energy requirements of an individual. The following are the rule-of-thumb figures for adults 20 through 50: to calculate your total daily energy consumption in calories, multiply your weight in pounds by 14 for a man and 13 for a woman if your lifestyle is largely sedentary; by 19 for a man and 17 for a woman if you are moderately active; and, by 23 for a man and 20 for a woman if you are very active. This amount of energy intake will maintain your current weight.

Age is an important factor. Children and adolescents who are still growing need enough calories to sustain their growth. However, once growth stops, the number of calories a body needs declines with age, even though body weight remains the same.

For example a 150 pound man who requires 2900 calories per day at age 25 will only need 2600 calories at age 45, and about 2100 calories at age 75 to maintain his weight and activity. This is why most of us wonder why we put on weight as we get older, even though we do not eat any more.

How many calories equal one pound?

One pound of body-weight is equivalent to about 3,500 calories. This means that if you consume 3,500 more calories than your body needs in a given period (a week or a month), you will gain one pound in weight;   conversely, if you consume 3,500 less calories than your body burns, you will lose one pound.

What is your ideal weight?

Your ideal weight depends on your sex, height and build. The table on the next page gives ranges of desirable weights for men and women of different heights. People with slender frames should weigh towards the lower end of the range;   people with large or stocky frames should weigh towards the top end of the range;   people with average frames, should weigh around the middle. The table is adapted from data prepared by Metropolitan Life Insurance Company; the height is with shoes, and weight is in indoor clothing.

   Before embarking on a weight loss or weight gain program, you should consult your physician. Your doctor should suggest your ideal weight, and the type of diet and exercise program you should undertake to achieve it.

Table of Desirable Weight for Men and Women

Height		Weight			
		Men		Women	
ft / in.	cm	lbs	kg	lbs	kg
4' 10"	147			92-119	42-54
4' 11"	150			94-122	43-55
5' 0"	152			96-125	44-57
5' 1"	155			99-128	45-58
5" 2"	157	112-141	51-64	102-131	46-59
5' 3"	160	115-144	52-65	105-134	48-61
5' 4"	163	118-148	54-67	108-138	49-63
5' 5"	165	121-152	55-69	111-142	50-64
5' 6"	168	124-156	56-71	114-146	52-66
5' 7"	170	128-161	58-73	118-150	53-68
5' 8"	173	132-166	60-75	122-154	55-70
5' 9"	175	136-170	62-77	126-158	57-72
5' 10"	178	140-174	64-79	130-163	59-74
5' 11"	180	144-179	65-81	134-168	61-76
6' 0"	183	148-184	67-83	138-173	63-78
6' 1"	185	152-189	69-86		
6' 2"	188	156-194	71-88		
6' 3"	191	160-199	73-90		
6' 4"	193	164-204	74-93		

Source: Adapted from Metropolitan Life Insurance Company data.

Understanding Dietary Cholesterol

Cholesterol is present in all foods of animal origin; that is, fish, meat and poultry products, dairy products, and eggs. Foods of plant origin, including vegetable oils, are always totally free of cholesterol.

Cholesterol content of food varies greatly. Generally, lean white meats have the least amount, and organ meats such as liver, kidney and brain have the highest. Below are some examples of the cholesterol content of raw and cooked (broiled, baked or boiled) foods:

Food	Cholest- erol raw	Cholest- erol cooked
Lean beef (3.5 oz or 100 gms)	61 mg	89 mg
Lean Lamb (3.5 oz)	66 mg	92 mg
Chicken breast meat without skin (3.5 oz)	58 mg	85 mg
Turkey breast meat without skin (3.5 oz)	60 mg	83 mg
Lamb Brain (3.5 oz)	1352 mg	2504 mg
Chicken Liver (3.5 oz)	439 mg	631 mg
Halibut (3.5 oz)	32 mg	41 mg
Shrimps (3.5 oz)	152 mg	195 mg
Egg (one large)	220 mg	220 mg
Whole milk (one 8-ounce cup)	35 mg	35 mg
Nonfat or skim milk (one 8-ounce cup)	4 mg	4 mg
Butter (1 ounce) (Cooked butter = ghee)	63 mg	73 mg

Source: USDA Handbook 8

Too much cholesterol in a diet tends to raise blood cholesterol in much the same way as saturated fat does. The American Heart Association advises that a blood cholesterol level of 200 milligrams per deciliter or higher poses a significant danger to heart health, causing accumulation of plaque in arteries which can lead to heart disease, stroke and their consequential problems.

Most doctors believe that the total blood cholesterol level should be below 180 milligrams per deciliter.

Dietary Goals

The American Heart Association has recommended that dietary cholesterol consumption for healthy individuals should be less than 300 milligrams per day. For persons who have elevated cholesterol levels, the recommended limit is 200 milligrams per day. Some doctors believe that a lower amount is preferable.

In practice, two servings of lean meat per day, with each serving limited to 4 ounces raw or 3 ounces cooked weight, plus two servings of nonfat milk products (for example, 2 cups of skim milk) would give you about 130 milligrams of cholesterol. This leaves some latitude for other foods such as shrimps or eggs now and again. Healthy individuals should limit their egg consumption to 3 whole eggs per week.

Please note that although there is little variation in cholesterol content of lean cuts of beef, lamb, chicken and turkey, the red meats such as lamb and beef and the darker parts of poultry have a higher content of saturated fats. These meats should, therefore, be consumed less often.

Understanding Food Labels - Buyer Beware

Food manufacturers use every degree of freedom that the law allows to make their packaging seduce the consumer into buying their products. The packaging includes "hype" statements, such as *100% cholesterol free, light, sugar free, low fat, all natural, etc.*, as well as the list of ingredients that make up the product. If the manufacturer makes any nutritional claims about the product, a nutritional analysis is also required.

For most of us, the problem arises from the bewildering array of names used to describe ingredients. If you do not understand these, then you do not know what you are buying or eating. For your own protection, become a knowledgeable label reader.

Information in this chapter describes labeling in the United States as required by law at the time of this writing. By the end of 1991, the Food and Drug Administration is expected to bring out regulations covering the use of words such as *light, low-fat, cholesterol free, low cholesterol,* etc. However, this legislation will not necessarily reduce the need for vigilance on the part of the consumer.

Lesson 1. Take it with a pinch of salt.

Ignore the "hype" statements; they are often meaningless and sometimes misleading. Below are examples of such statements:

Some meaningless or misleading labels:
• All Natural
• Fresh
• Low Fat
• Sugar Free
• Light or Lite
• Ninety-something per cent fat free
• 100% Cholesterol Free

The following terms do have a meaning under the current law:

Low-calorie: No more than 40 calories per serving or 0.4 calories per gram.

Reduced Calorie: Has at least 1/3 fewer calories than the food it replaces without affecting its nutritional value. (Note: This does not mean that the food is "low-calorie.")

Sodium-free: Has less than 5 mg of sodium per serving.

Very low sodium: Has no more than 35 mg of sodium per serving.

Low sodium: Has no more than 140 mg of sodium per serving.

Reduced sodium: Has at least 75% less sodium than the food it replaces.

Lesson 2. Ingredients by any other name.

Learn what the list of ingredients means:

1. Ingredients are listed in descending order of amount by weight, that is, the ingredient in the largest quantity is listed first.

2. Ingredients described by different names fall into a number of main categories such as fat, sugar, sodium, preservatives, color, flavor, etc.

Some Different Names used for Fat:

- Animal Fats*
- Butter*
- Cream Solids*
- Fat (Lard, Chicken, Beef, etc.)*
- Hydrogenated or Partially Hydrogenated Oil or Shortening*
- Lecithin
- Margarine*
- Oil (canola, soybean, corn, etc.)
- Oil (coconut, palm, palm kernel, etc.)*
- Tropical Oils*

*Note: These fats have a high saturated content; fats of animal origin also contain cholesterol.

Some Different Names for Sugars

- Corn sweeteners
- Corn Syrup
- Dextrose
- Fructose
- Glucose
- Honey
- Maltose
- Mannitol
- Molasses
- Sorbitol
- Sucrose
- Sugar (cane, beet, brown, invert, etc.)
- Turnibado

Some names of ingredients with high Sodium content:

- Baking powder
- Baking soda
- Disodium phosphate
- Kelp
- Monosodium glutamate or MSG
- Salt
- Sea salt
- Sodium benzoate
- Sodium bicarbonate
- Sodium chloride

To show what you may find in a supermarket, an example of the list of ingredients for a product (say, Product X) is shown below:

Product X

Ingredients: Whole wheat, rolled oats, sugar, brown sugar, partially hydrogenated soybean and/or coconut oil, malted barley, salt, corn syrup, honey, artificial flavor, artificial food coloring (Yellow No, 5), BHT, MSG.

Lesson 3. What's in a Serving

Nutritional information for Product X may look like this:

Product X	
Serving Size	1 ounce
Calories	110
Protein	2 gms
Carbohydrates	23 gms
Total Fat	6 gms
Polyunsaturated fatty acid	4 gms
Saturated fatty acid	2 gms
Cholesterol	0 mg
Sodium	180 mg

Carbohydrate information may also be given:

Product X	
Dietary fiber	1 g
Complex carbohydrates	16 g
Sucrose and other sugars	6 g
Total carbohydrates	23 g

The following points should be noted about the nutritional information:

- Nutrient values on labels are approximate (to within $\pm 20\%$)
- *Serving size* does not necessarily represent a typical serving. The amount you actually eat could as easily be two or more *servings* as defined on the package. The calories, fat, etc. that you actually consume should be calculated accordingly.
- To work out fat and saturated fat calories, multiply total fat and saturated fat in grams by 9.

Total fat calories: $6 \times 9 = 54$ calories ($= 49\%$ of total calories)
Saturated fat calories: $2 \times 9 = 18$ calories ($= 16\%$ of total calories)

Start reading labels. The supermarket is where good eating habits begin.

Understanding the Makings of a Balanced Diet

To help people plan a balanced diet, the U.S. Department of Agriculture has divided all foods into five groups, with a recommendation of the number of servings to be consumed every day from each group:

Group 1.   Fruit and Vegetable Group
4 or more servings per day

1 serving equals, for example:
1/2 cup fruit or vegetable
1/2 cup fruit or vegetable juice
1/4 cup dried fruit
1 medium apple, orange, banana

Group 2.   Grain Group: Breads, cereals and other grains
4 or more servings per day

1 serving equals, for example:
1/2 cup cooked rice, pasta, cereal
1 chapati, tortilla
1 slice bread
1/2 hamburger bun, muffin

Group 3.   Milk Group: Milk and milk products
Adults: 2 servings per day
Children: 3 to 4 servings per day
Pregnant and lactating women: 4 servings per day

1 serving equals, for example:
1 cup milk
1 cup yogurt
1 ounce cheese
1/2 cup ice milk, frozen yogurt
1/2 cup cottage cheese

Group 4.　　　　Poultry, fish, meat, eggs, legumes, nuts and seeds
　　　　　　　　2 servings per day

　　　　　　　　1 serving equals, for example:
　　　　　　　　　　3 oz cooked (4 oz uncooked) meat,
　　　　　　　　　　poultry or fish
　　　　　　　　　　1/2 cup cooked lentils, daals, dried peas
　　　　　　　　　　or beans
　　　　　　　　　　1 egg

Group 5.　　　　Fats, Sugar, Sweets, and Alcohol
　　　　　　　　No recommended number of servings

To achieve a balanced diet you should eat a wide variety of foods from the first four basic food groups. Do not exceed the recommended number of servings from Group 4 (the meat group). The stated number of servings will give you about 1200 calories. For additional calories that you require to maintain your ideal weight, eat foods mainly from Groups 1 and 2 (the fruit and vegetable group, and the grain group), and   as little as possible from Group 5 (the fats, sweets and alcohol group).

Analyzing Your Daily Diet

A balanced and healthful diet depends on what you consume in a whole day, and not just on the nutritional value of individual dishes. If you wish to analyze your daily diet, an example of how to do so is given on page 264 for an adult who is allowed 2000 calories per day. This example is designed to show how you can figure out whether your day's diet is balanced and whether it meets your specific dietary guidelines.

To analyze your own daily diet, base the analysis on the foods you eat. Construct a table similar to the one on page 264, record everything you eat on each day, list nutrient values of these foods, and add them up as in the summary table below. To work out approximate percentage contributions of the different nutrients, remember that one gram of protein or carbohydrates yields about 4 calories, and one gram of fat yields about 9 calories.

You won't have to play this numbers game for the rest of your life; once you get an idea of what makes a good daily diet, eating healthfully will become your second nature.

A summary of the analysis of the day's diet illustrated on page 264 is as follows:

Nutrient Analysis (for the day)

Total calories	2030	goal: 2000
Protein	107 gms	20% of total calories
Carbohydrates	349 gms	67% of total calories
Total Fat	30 gms	13% of total calories
Saturated Fat	3 gms	1% of total calories
Cholesterol	80 mg	goal: less than 300
Sodium	2080 mg	goal: less than 3000

An Example of a 2000-calorie Balanced Diet

Meals and servings	Cal	Prot gm	Car gm	Fat gm	Sat Fat	Cho mg	Na mg
Breakfast:							
4-oz Orange Juice	56	1	13	0	0	0	1
1 Shredded Wheat Biscuit	90	2	19	1	0	0	1
1/2 cup Nonfat milk	43	4	6	0	0	2	63
1 tsp Sugar	15	0	4	0	0	0	0
1 serving Omelette*	99	12	8	3	0	0	305
1 Chapati*	106	4	20	3	0	0	1
1 cup tea w/ 1 tbsp nonfat milk	7	1	1	0	0	0	8
Mid-morning Snack:							
1 Apple (5 oz)	81	0	21	0	0	0	0
Lunch:							
1 Tuna Sandwich*	207	16	31	4	1	16	375
1 Serving Coleslaw*	40	1	10	0	0	0	103
Grapes (10)	36	0	9	0	0	0	1
1 cup nonfat milk	86	8	12	0	0	4	126
Afternoon snack:							
2 Nankhatai*	174	3	26	6	1	0	91
1 cup tea w/ 1 tbsp nonfat milk	7	1	1	0	0	0	8
Dinner:							
1 serving Salad with Lemon Dressing*	26	1	6	0	0	0	99
1/2 serving Mixed Vegetable Curry*	66	2	11	2	0	0	110
1 Chapati*	106	4	20	3	0	0	1
1 serving Turkey Kabab Curry*	285	27	30	7	1	56	284
1 serving Plain Rice*	211	4	46	0	0	0	269
1 serving Nonfat Kesar Kulfi*	98	7	16	0	0	4	107
Bed-time snack:							
1 Banana (4 oz)	105	1	27	1	0	0	1
1 cup nonfat milk	86	8	12	0	0	4	126
Totals	2030	107	349	30	3	80	2080

Cal = Calories
Car = Carbohydrates
Cho = Cholesterol
Na = Sodium
Prot = Protein
Sat. = Saturated

Note: All numbers are rounded to the nearest 0.5. Numbers marked as 0 indicate that the quantity of the corresponding nutrient is either zero, or that it is negligible.
* indicates a dish made from a recipe in this book

The meals listed in the table on the opposite page provide a balanced diet according to the number of servings of the four basic food groups, as illustrated in the table below:

Analysis by food groups:

Fruit and vegetables group	6 servings
Grain Group	6 servings
Protein Group (meat, lentils, etc)	2 servings
Milk group	3 servings

Painless Transition to a Healthful Diet

Nobody really likes change. It is uncomfortable and annoying. This is precisely why this book was written. If health care demands a change, then the less drastic it is the better. For people who normally eat Indian food, this book offers an alternative to making drastic changes in their diet. However, healthful living will still require changes to old and established habits.

Sudden changes always cause the greatest problems. Therefore, unless you are advised by your physician to adopt a new diet immediately, you and your family might find it more acceptable to make changes over a period of time.

The chapter entitled "About Recipes in this Book" on page 12 outlines how recipes in this book were modified and suggests how you can follow these same principles to modify your own favorite dishes. It concentrates on five major areas.

First, if you are a non-vegetarian, then eat mainly fish, and poultry with skin and all visible fat removed. But limit servings to eight ounces (raw weight) per day. It would be good to skip meat now and again and obtain your protein from legumes instead. Your family is unlikely to object to this change too much. If you enjoy eating beef and lamb, you don't have to give up red meat entirely. Very lean beef and lamb are alright once in a while.

Second, cook only with acceptable vegetable oils. This means butter and ghee are out. You may have to give up certain dishes, but that still leaves you scores of other dishes to choose from instead. This is really a small price to pay for the benefit of good health.

Third, cook with less oil and fat. Using less fat will alter the appearance of a dish a little bit and people who like the taste of fat on their tongues will miss it for a short while, but they will soon get used to the new taste. Try the recipes in this book, they are low fat but still delicious. Also cut down on fried foods, most of which contain a disproportionate number of fat calories. (Please see "Tips on Reducing Oil in Fried Foods" on page 268).

Fourth, reduce salt. This is where you may notice a big change. By using lemon juice and/or yogurt in savory dishes, you will largely make up for the decreased saltiness. However, you may reduce salt over a period of time; for example, by about a fifth or a quarter every month. This allows the tongue to become accustomed to less salty tastes gradually and imperceptibly. Eventually you will find that you enjoy food even more because those natural flavors in food which get masked by salt begin to come through.

Fifth, switch to non-fat dairy products. People who are used to drinking whole milk will notice the greatest difference. The human tongue takes about three weeks to get used to new tastes and textures. So if you drink whole milk now, change to 2% low-fat milk first. A month later replace 2% with 1% low-fat milk and then eventually with nonfat milk. Believe me, once your family becomes accustomed to the refreshing taste of skim milk, they will hate the sticky creaminess of fatty milk. But please don't give up milk; it is an essential supplier of calcium, and even adults should consume two servings of dairy products a day. (Please read "Understanding the Makings of a Balanced Diet" on page 261).

As to other dairy products: changing to nonfat yogurt for cooking or eating is not too noticeable; people who like ice cream should try Ice Milk or, better still, nonfat frozen yogurt; for cheese lovers, the dairy industry is now beginning to introduce low-fat cheeses with acceptable tastes.

If you change things at your table gradually, your family will hardly notice it. A switch-over period of six months is fine. However, do not give up the process half-way through. It is too easy to lose the way, and your health is far too important for that.

Tips on Reducing Oil in Fried Foods

Most fried foods contain far too much fat than is good in a healthful diet. However, since complete deprivation never works, one is likely to continue eating fried snacks such as potato chips. Indians love snacks such as *Chevdo, Sev, Ganthia*, and a host of others; all of them delicious and, unfortunately, deep fried.

A way to get rid of some of the fat ingrained in these snacks (potato chips included) is to store them in a square or an oblong container in layers, between sheets of absorbent paper towel. You will be amazed at the amount of fat which is absorbed by the paper towels -- that is the amount of extra fat you would have otherwise consumed.

When you deep fry foods at home, drain them in a tray or colander lined with paper towels. This method also helps to absorb excess oil.

Another category of foods that Indians are very fond of are sweets, such as *Ladoo*. These are loaded with butter and sugar and have no place in a good diet. However, some of these dishes can be made with acceptable vegetable oils. Even these should be eaten only very occasionally. A way to reduce fat from these dishes is, first, to store them between layers of paper towels, and second, just before eating, to heat them in a microwave oven which softens them, and finally to wrap them in a paper towel and squeeze out as much fat as possible. This will break up your *ladoo* but it will also take away a lot of fat.

Eating Out

Necessary and pleasurable as it may be, eating out can be the greatest saboteur of a healthful diet. The biggest problem is for people who eat out when at work. For them, it is almost an economic necessity to patronize inexpensive fast-food restaurants. The food they serve is called 'junk food' with good reason. The best thing for such individuals would be to take packed meals from home; the next best thing would be to select foods which are least bad. Many fast-food outlets are beginning to offer such items as salads, broiled skinless chicken-breast sandwiches and lowfat desserts. Choose from amongst these. Supplement this diet with fresh fruits and vegetables. Then make sure that you balance out the excesses of outside meals by eating extra-healthy food at home. This advice also applies to children who eat school meals.

For people who dine out for pleasure, the problem can be less acute, unless they eat out often. First, patronize only those restaurants whose cuisines are acceptable -- for example, classical French cuisine with its rich buttery sauces would hardly qualify. Second, ask the server to suggest the type of dishes which suit your diet. Good restaurants, which prepare food to order, are always happy to cook to your specification. When my husband and I go out, say to a Chinese restaurant, we always specify that we want our food stir fried in only a little oil, with no MSG, less salt, and served with steamed rice. In Indian restaurants, Tandoori dishes are safest. In a western restaurant, broiled meats and fish simply cooked with herbs and spices, and accompanied by vegetables without butter, are most delicious and perfectly healthful. Remove skin from chicken before eating. Also remove any visible fat from meat and poultry. Order sauces and dressings on the side. Never be shy about specifying what you want. If the restaurant is not willing to oblige, go somewhere else.

One of the favorite pleasures for Indians is eating sweets such as *Ladoo, Burfi, Halwa, Monthaar, Jalebi, Ras Malai*, etc. These delectable dishes are unfortunately very rich in butter (*ghee*), whole milk products and sugar. These delights, eaten out or at home, can easily destroy the balance in your diet. Eat these dishes very infrequently and sparingly.

And, very occasionally, if you lapse, enjoy without guilt. You can always make up for it at the next meal.

Understanding Coronary Risk Factors

Heart disease is the single biggest killer in western industrialized countries; more people die of heart diseases in the United States than due to all other causes combined. The following are identified by the medical community as the major factors which significantly increase a persons chances of suffering a heart attack; the presence of more than one risk factor produces a multifold increase in the risk of having a heart attack.

- High total blood cholesterol level
- Low level of 'good' (HDL) cholesterol
- Cigarette smoking
- High blood pressure
- Male sex
- A family or previous history of heart attack
- Diabetes
- Obesity (30% or more overweight)
- Stress
- Lack of physical activity or exercise

You can't do anything about being male, or your genes, or the family's or your personal previous history of heart attack, but you *can* do something about all the other factors through personal effort and/or professional medical assistance. (Please note that although women are statistically at lower risk in younger years, the risk begins to approach that of men after menopause. Therefore, being female is not a reason to be carefree).

Abnormal cholesterol levels, high blood pressure and diabetes are silent diseases; that is, they do not produce any symptoms until some damage is done to the body. The only way to find out about the presence of these risk factors is to have regular medical check-ups.

If any of the listed risk factors are present, you should be guided by your physician. In most cases, diet, exercise, weight control, refraining from smoking and stress management are the primary lines of defense. When these alone do not work, your doctor may prescribe medication to complement your efforts.

Don't let a heart attack surprise you. You *can* do something to beat the odds.

Nutrient Values of Common Foods

The following pages contain Nutrient Values of commonly used foods in the following categories:

- Dairy products
- Eggs
- Fats and Oils
- Fish, Meat and Poultry
- Fruits and Fruit Juices
- Grain products
- Nuts
- Peas and Beans
- Sugars
- Vegetables

These foods are commonly used for cooking and eating. The nutrient analysis will help you in determining the nutrient values of foods you use, in analyzing recipes, and in analyzing your daily diet as discussed on page 263.

The following sources have been used in constructing these tables:

- USDA Handbook 8
- Canadian Nutrient File
- Manufacturers' data

Apart from generic data on processed foods such as dairy products, margarines and breads, no data is given on manufactured foods (such as cereals, cookies, cakes, canned foods, etc.) or 'fast foods' (such as those available in restaurant chains, for example McDonald's, Burger King, Pizza Hut, etc.). There is a wide variation in nutrient values of foods manufactured by different companies, and manufacturers also modify their products from time to time. For such foods, the most reliable data will be obtained by reading packaging labels (see page 257). Major fast food restaurant chains will usually provide nutrient analysis of their menu items on request.

DAIRY PRODUCTS

Food/Portion Size	Weight gm	Energy Calories	Energy kJoule	Protein gm	Carbo gm	Fat gm	Sat. Fat gm	Chol. mg	Sodium mg
Cheese									
Cheddar (1 oz)	28	113	472	7	0	9	6	29	174
Cottage Low fat 2% (1 cup)	226	203	848	31	8	4	3	19	918
Cottage Low fat 1% (1 cup)	226	163	685	28	6	2	1	10	918
Cottage Nonfat (1 cup)	226	140	585	30	6	0	0	10	660
Cream (1 oz)	28	98	409	2	1	10	6	31	83
Mozzarella Part skim milk (1 oz)	28	71	298	7	1	4	3	16	131
Ricotta Part skim milk (1 oz)	28	39	162	3	1	2	1	8	35
Cream									
Light - Unwhipped (1 tbsp)	15	44	184	tr	tr	5	3	17	5
Heavy - Unwhipped (1 tbsp)	15	51	216	tr	tr	6	4	21	6
Sour cream (1 tbsp)	12	26	108	tr	tr	3	2	5	6
Fats									
Butter w/o salt (1 tbsp=1/2 oz)	14	100	418	0	0	11	7	31	2
Butter w/salt (1 tbsp=1/2 oz)	14	100	418	0	0	11	7	31	116
Ghee (1 tbsp=1/2 oz)	14	123	513	0	0	14	9	36	0
Milk									
Whole - 3.7% fat (1 cup)	244	157	655	8	11	9	6	35	119
Low fat - 2% fat (1 cup)	246	137	572	10	14	5	3	19	145
Low fat - 1 % fat (1 cup)	246	119	499	10	14	3	2	10	143
Nonfat - skim (1 cup)	246	100	418	10	14	1	tr	5	144
Evaporated, unswtnd, whole (1 C)	252	339	1417	17	25	19	12	74	267
Evaporated, unswtnd, skim (1 cup)	256	200	835	19	29	1	tr	9	294
Condensed, sweetened (1 cup)	306	982	4108	24	166	27	17	104	389
Dry Powder, nonfat (1 cup)	68	246	1029	25	35	1	tr	13	364

Food/Portion Size	Weight gm	Energy Calories	Energy kJoule	Protein gm	Carbo gm	Fat gm	Sat. Fat gm	Chol. mg	Sodium mg
Yogurt									
Plain, whole milk (1 cup)	227	139	583	8	11	7	5	29	105
Low fat - 2% (1 cup)	227	143	601	12	16	4	3	14	159
Nonfat (1 cup)	227	127	530	13	17	tr	tr	4	174
Frozen Desserts									
Ice cream - Rich 16% fat (1 cup)	148	349	1462	4	32	24	15	88	108
Ice milk 3% fat (1 cup)	175	184	769	5	29	6	4	105	18
Frozen Yogurt, Low fat (1 cup)	226	246	1028	12	37	5	3	18	120
EGGS									
Whole, raw (1 egg)	50	75	313	6	1	5	2	220	63
White, raw (1 white)	33	17	69	4	tr	0	0	0	55
yolk, raw (1 yolk)	17	59	249	3	tr	5	2	220	8
FATS AND OILS									
Margarine - corn oil (1 tbsp)	14	100	418	0	tr	11	2	0	151
Margarine, diet (1 tbsp)	14	50	209	0	tr	6	1	0	138
Oils (1 tbsp)	14	124	518	0	0	see	page	# 248	0
FISH, MEAT AND POULTRY									
Fin Fish									
Cod (3.5 oz raw)	100	82	344	18	0	1	tr	43	54
Haddock (3.5 oz raw)	100	87	365	19	0	1	tr	57	68
Halibut (3.5 oz raw)	100	110	458	21	0	2	tr	32	54
Salmon (3.5 oz raw)	100	142	594	20	0	6	1	55	44
Trout (3.5 oz raw)	100	148	620	21	0	7	1	58	52
Tuna - canned in oil w/ salt (3.5 oz)	100	198	830	29	0	8	2	18	354
Tuna - canned in water w/o salt	100	131	547	30	0	1	tr	18	50

Food/Portion Size	Weight gm	Energy Calories	Energy kJoule	Protein gm	Carbo gm	Fat gm	Sat. Fat gm	Chol. mg	Sodium mg
Shell Fish									
Clams (3.5 oz raw)	100	74	309	13	3	1	tr	34	56
Crabmeat (3.5 oz raw)	100	84	349	18	0	1	tr	42	836
Lobster (3.5 oz raw)	100	90	378	18	1	1	tr	95	296
Shrimp (3.5 oz raw)	100	106	444	20	1	2	tr	152	148
Meat									
Beef, lean (3.5 oz raw)	100	136	569	21	0	5	2	61	58
Beef, ground, extra ln, (3.5 oz raw)	100	234	980	19	0	17	7	69	66
Beef, ground, regular (3.5 oz raw)	100	310	1299	17	0	27	11	85	68
Lamb, lean (3.5 oz raw)	100	130	543	20	0	5	3	70	70
Pork, lean (3.5 oz raw)	100	151	631	21	0	7	2	63	50
Pork, Bacon (3.5 oz raw)	100	556	2328	9	0	58	21	67	730
Veal, lean (3.5 oz raw)	100	107	447	21	0	2	1	78	64
Poultry (raw)									
Chicken breast, meat only (3.5 oz)	100	110	459	23	0	1	tr	58	65
Chicken Drumsticks, meat only	100	119	497	21	0	3	1	77	88
Chicken Thighs, meat only, (3.5 oz)	100	119	497	20	0	4	1	83	86
Duck, meat and skin (3.5 oz)	100	211	885	17	0	15	5	80	56
Duck, meat only (3.5 oz)	100	132	551	18	0	6	2	77	74
Turkey breast, meat only (3.5 oz)	100	111	464	25	0	1	tr	62	49
Turkey, dark meat (3.5 oz)	100	111	464	20	0	3	1	81	69
FRUITS									
Apples (1 about 5 oz)	138	81	338	tr	21	1	tr	0	0
Apricots (3 about 4 oz)	106	51	213	2	12	tr	tr	0	1
Avocados (1 about 7 oz flesh)	201	370	1550	5	17	35	6	0	23
Bananas (1 about 4 oz flesh)	114	105	437	1	27	1	tr	0	1

Food/Portion Size	Weight gm	Energy Calories	Energy kjoule	Protein gm	Carbo gm	Fat gm	Sat. Fat gm	Chol. mg	Sodium mg
FRUITS (continued)									
Cantaloupe (1/2 fruit, about 10 oz)	267	94	395	2	22	1	tr	0	24
Cherries (10)	68	49	204	1	11	1	tr	0	0
Figs (1 medium, about 2 oz)	50	37	155	tr	10	tr	tr	0	1
Grapefruit (1/2 fruit about 4 oz)	118	39	165	1	10	tr	tr	0	0
Grapes (10 about 2 oz)	50	36	149	tr	9	tr	tr	0	1
Kiwifruit (1 large, about 3 oz)	91	56	231	1	14	tr	0	0	5
Mangos (1 fruit about 7.5 oz)	207	135	565	1	35	1	0	0	4
Honeydew melon (6 0z)	170	59	251	1	16	tr	0	0	17
Oranges (1 fruit about 4.5 oz)	131	62	258	1	15	tr	tr	0	0
Papaya (1/2 fruit about 5.5 oz)	152	59	245	1	15	tr	tr	0	5
Peaches (1 fruit about 3 oz)	87	37	156	1	10	tr	tr	0	0
Pears (1 fruit about 6 oz)	166	98	410	1	25	1	tr	0	0
Pineapple (1 slice about 3 oz)	84	41	174	tr	10	tr	tr	0	1
Strawberries (1cup about 5 oz)	149	45	189	1	10	1	tr	0	1
Watermelon (about 6 oz)	160	51	211	1	12	1	tr	0	3
DRIED FRUIT									
Apricots (1/2 cup about 2 oz)	60	192	803	3	50	tr	tr	0	8
Dates (10 fruits about 3 oz)	83	228	955	2	61	tr	tr	0	2
Figs (10 fruits about 7 oz)	187	477	1997	6	122	2	tr	0	21
Raisins (1 cup about 5 oz)	145	435	1817	5	115	1	tr	0	17
FRUIT JUICES									
Apple juice, unsweetened (1 cup)	248	117	486	tr	29	tr	tr	0	7
Grapefruit juice, unswtnd (1 cup)	247	94	390	1	22	tr	tr	0	2
Grape juice (1 cup)	253	154	648	1	38	tr	tr	0	8
Orange juice (1 cup)	248	112	464	2	26	tr	tr	0	2
Pineapple juice, unswtnd (1 cup)	250	140	583	1	34	tr	tr	0	3

GRAIN PRODUCTS

Food/Portion Size	Weight gm	Energy Calories	Energy kjoule	Protein gm	Carbo gm	Fat gm	Sat. Fat gm	Chol. mg	Sodium mg
Breads									
White bread (1 slice)	23	63	263	2	12	1	tr	0	113
Whole wheat bread (1 slice)	23	56	234	2	11	1	tr	0	121
Grains and Flours									
All-purpose flour (1 cup)	125	455	1906	13	95	1	tr	0	3
Bulgur (1 cup)	140	496	2073	16	106	2	0	0	6
Cream of wheat (1 cup)	167	601	2518	21	122	2	tr	0	2
Millet (1 cup)	200	756	3166	22	146	8	1	0	10
Oat bran (1/2 cup)	47	116	484	8	31	3	1	0	2
Pasta, dry (2 oz uncooked)	57	211	885	7	43	1	tr	0	4
Rice - long grain (1 cup)	185	675	2829	13	148	1	tr	0	9
Rice flour (1 cup)	158	578	2417	9	127	2	1	0	7
Whole wheat flour (1 cup)	120	407	1704	16	87	2	tr	0	6
NUTS									
Almonds, dried (1 oz)	28	167	700	6	6	15	1	0	3
Brazil Nuts, dried (1 oz)	28	186	780	4	4	19	5	0	1
Cashew nuts, dry roasted (1 oz)	28	163	682	4	9	13	3	0	5
Chestnuts, roasted (1 oz)	28	239	998	5	52	1	tr	0	4
Coconut meat, desiccated (1 oz)	28	187	784	2	7	18	16	0	11
Coconut meat, raw (1 oz)	28	99	414	1	4	10	8	0	6
Macadamia Nuts, dried (1 oz)	28	199	834	2	4	21	3	0	1
Peanuts , oil roasted (1 oz)	28	165	690	7	5	14	2	0	4
Pistachios, dry roasted (1 oz)	28	172	720	4	8	15	2	0	2
Walnuts, English, dried (1 oz)	28	182	763	4	5	18	2	0	2

Food/Portion Size	Weight gm	Energy Calories	Energy kjoule	Protein gm	Carbo gm	Fat gm	Sat. Fat gm	Chol. mg	Sodium mg
PEAS AND BEANS									
Black-eyed (cow) peas (1 cup)	167	561	2351	39	100	2	1	0	27
Chickpeas or Garbanzo (1 cup)	200	728	3050	39	121	12	1	0	48
Kidney beans, all types (1 cup)	184	613	2563	43	110	2	tr	0	44
Lentils (1 cup)	192	649	2713	54	110	2	tr	0	19
Lima beans (1 cup)	178	601	2518	38	113	1	tr	0	32
Mung beans (1 cup)	207	718	3008	49	130	2	1	0	31
SUGARS									
Honey (1 tsp)	7	21	88	0	6	0	0	0	tr
Sugar-Brown (1 tsp not packed)	5	17	71	0	6	0	0	0	2
Sugar-White granulated (1 tsp)	4	15	64	0	4	0	0	0	tr
Sugar-White powdered (1 cup)	120	462	1931	0	119	0	0	0	1
VEGETABLES									
Beans -green, raw (3.5 oz)	100	31	129	2	7	tr	tr	0	6
Carrots, raw (3.5 oz)	100	43	181	1	10	tr	tr	0	35
Celery, raw (3.5 oz)	100	16	67	1	4	tr	tr	0	87
Coriander (Cilantro), raw (3.5 oz)	100	20	83	2	3	tr	tr	0	28
Corn, yellow (kernels from 1 ear)	90	77	322	3	17	1	tr	0	14
Garlic, raw (3.5 oz)	100	149	623	6	33	1	tr	0	17
Ginger root (3.5 oz)	100	69	287	2	15	1	tr	0	13
Onions, raw (3.5 oz)	100	38	158	1	8	tr	tr	0	3
Peas, green, raw (3.5 oz)	100	81	339	5	14	tr	tr	0	5
Potatoes, raw (3.5 oz)	100	79	331	2	18	tr	tr	0	6
Spinach, raw (3.5 oz)	100	22	94	3	4	tr	tr	0	79
Most other vegetables, raw, 3.5 oz	100	13-30	50-125	1-3	3-8	tr	tr	0	2-30

Index